The Tree
in the
Churchyard

A Bicentennial History of
Meadow Creek Presbyterian Church

RUTH KROSS

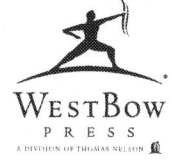

WESTBOW
PRESS
A DIVISION OF THOMAS NELSON

Scripture references in the Forward were taken from the Holy Bible, New International Version. Copyright 1973, 1978, 1984 by International Bible Society. Used by permission of Zondervan. All rights reserved.

Scripture references in book taken from Harper Study Bible, Revised Standard Version. Copyright 1962 by Concordance, Harper and Row, Publishers. Used by permission. All rights reserved.

Quotation from Calvin's Institutes taken from John T. McNeill's edited version, Calvin: Institutes of the Christian Religion. Philadelphia: The Westminster Press, 1960.

WestBow Press books may be ordered through booksellers or by contacting:

WestBow Press
A Division of Thomas Nelson
1663 Liberty Drive
Bloomington, IN 47403
www.westbowpress.com
1-(866) 928-1240

Because of the dynamic nature of the Internet, any web addresses or links contained in this book may have changed since publication and may no longer be valid. The views expressed in this work are solely those of the author and do not necessarily reflect the views of the publisher, and the publisher hereby disclaims any responsibility for them.

Any people depicted in stock imagery provided by Thinkstock are models, and such images are being used for illustrative purposes only.
Certain stock imagery © Thinkstock.

ISBN: 978-1-4497-3886-0 (hc)
ISBN: 978-1-4497-3887-7 (sc)
ISBN: 978-1-4497-3888-4 (e)
Library of Congress Control Number: 2012901535

Printed in the United States of America
WestBow Press rev. date: 02/09/2012

Table of Contents

Chapter One.........*Planting the Seed*

Chapter Two.........*The Ways of the Lord*

Chapter Three......*Branches of God's Family Tree*

Chapter Four.........Programs and Plans

Hard Working Women *114*
Keeping the Acorns Close to the Tree *119*

Appendices

It is a magnificent red oak.

At the base of its trunk, it is seventy-four inches in diameter.

Its estimated height is ninety feet and its roots extend deeply into the clay soil of Tennessee. Those roots are firmly anchored, and it has withstood many storms.

The branches extend out in all directions.

Mike Smith of the Tennessee Department of Forestry estimated its age to be about 200 years and diagnosed its condition as "very healthy."

To the west of the tree is a large cemetery containing the remains of many family members of the church. The story of Meadow Creek is the story of God's covenant promises to generations of these faithful people.

The church is a simple, red-brick country church, constructed in 1929, the third sanctuary built on the site.

Many members of the church have roots that extend all the way back to the pioneer past of Tennessee. They are firmly anchored in the Word of God. As a body of believers, they have withstood many storms.

Established in 1812, the church is also 200 years old.

Its condition is "Blessed by the Hand of God."

Foreword by Rev. Jeff Neikirk

When my wife and I first visited Meadow Creek in early 2008, we were struck by just how different it was going to be to minister to the small congregation that God gathered together in an old brick church that sat beside a towering oak tree.

As a church member gave us a tour of the area, I remember thinking, "Man, this church is in the middle of nowhere." It's not really that the church is far removed from civilization; it's just that it is very different from the Florida county we came from—one million people living within 274 square miles. Compare that to Greene County, where Meadow Creek is located: over 624 square miles, with less than 70,000 residents.

But that was just one of the first impressions that struck us. While Florida is home to one of the oldest settlements in the United States (St. Augustine), the state has very little history, as most of Florida's growth happened in the last fifty years. Most of the churches we belonged to in Florida were new church plants, with no history and no tradition. God, in his wisdom, decided to bring us to a church with a 200 year history and a long tradition, including generations of families who have been a part of the church for most, if not all, of its existence. Florida is so transient that the church sometimes seems to have a revolving door, but here in Greene County, families have stayed on the land their forefathers owned for generations, and they stay in the church, as well.

This is the legacy of a church like Meadow Creek: families—families who were there to support and love one another through thick and thin; families who raised up the next generation to work their land, and to love the Lord their God. In a real sense, families were non-existent in Florida. People had their immediate family, but for most, grandparents, great grandparents, aunts and uncles, and cousins, all lived in other states. At Meadow Creek, we found families and extended families, whose histories are intertwined with the history of the 200 year old church located at the edge of the mountains in east Tennessee.

The story that *The Tree In The Churchyard* tells is the story of families, and how God worked through those families to build a church. It is only fitting that the story of Meadow Creek is intertwined with the story of families, because not only are families the building blocks of society, but throughout history God has worked through families to accomplish His purposes, too. Think about all the pages in the Bible that are dedicated to family lines and genealogies. God works through families! How did the ark get built? It was Noah and his sons, and it was his family that was saved through his obedience (Genesis 6). What was the promise God made to Abraham when he called Abraham to leave Ur of the Chaldeans?

Genesis 17:7 *I will establish my covenant as an everlasting covenant between me and you and your descendants after you for the generations to come, to be your God and the God of your descendants after you.*

As God sent Moses to lead the Israelites out of Egypt, He told Moses to tell them this:

Exodus 3:15 *God also said to Moses, "Say to the Israelites, 'The LORD, the God of your fathers—the God of Abraham, the God of Isaac and the God of Jacob—has sent me to you.' This is my name forever, the name by which I am to be remembered from generation to generation.*

From these early accounts of God interacting with people we see that God is a covenant-keeping God who loves to work through families. It was families who were given the task of instructing their children concerning their relationship with God (Deuteronomy 6:3-12). As David ruled as king over Israel, God once again chose to work through families, and He promised David that someone from David's family would always rule over Israel (2 Samuel 7:11-16), a promise that was fulfilled when Jesus left the throne room of heaven and came to dwell on earth (Matthew 1:1-16).

Matthew 1:1-16 *A record of the genealogy of Jesus Christ the son of David, the son of Abraham: ² Abraham was the father of Isaac, Isaac the father of Jacob . . . ⁶ and Jesse the father of King David. David was the father of Solomon, whose mother had been Uriah's wife . . . ¹⁶ and Jacob the father of Joseph, the husband of Mary, of whom was born Jesus, who is called Christ.*

Throughout the Old Testament, God providentially worked through families to carry out his wonderful plan to redeem a fallen world. Even in the New Testament, as the early church became established, God continued to work through families.

Acts 2:37-39 *When the people heard this, they were cut to the heart and said to Peter and the other apostles, "Brothers, what shall we do?"* [38] *Peter replied, "Repent and be baptized, every one of you, in the name of Jesus Christ for the forgiveness of your sins. And you will receive the gift of the Holy Spirit.* [39] **The promise is for you and your children** *and for all who are far off—for all whom the Lord our God will call."*

It shouldn't surprise us then to know that God is still working through families when we hear the stories of God's redeeming work in a little church in the hills of east Tennessee. *The Tree In The Churchyard* recounts the stories of those families and how God has worked in and through them for 200 years to accomplish His purpose of redeeming a fallen world.

Preface

My husband and I moved to Greene County, Tennessee, in 1998. We were "empty-nesters." He built our home on Gregg Mill Road and I immersed myself in the history of the area. We first attended services at Meadow Creek Presbyterian Church in early 1999. We soon felt at home.

In the spring of 2006 Janice Hoyle and Virginia Waddell asked me to help them map the cemetery and update the cemetery directory. It was a lot of work. While we worked we discussed the families represented there and speculated on their lives. It took us eighteen months to finish this project.

In 2009 we started thinking about the bicentennial of our little church. We decided to try and write its history. We began by re-reading the "Blue-Book," a history written in 1987 in honor of the 175th anniversary. Then we read the history of the Timber Ridge Presbyterian Church and local histories written by Goldene Burgner and Mitzi Bible. In the meantime, I continued working at my two part-time jobs: teaching history at Tusculum College and serving as a tour guide for Main Street Greeneville. Both of those jobs enabled me to study more about the First Frontier, Andrew Johnson, Davy Crockett, the Civil War, and life in the Southern Appalachians.

In 2010 we began conducting oral histories of the members of Meadow Creek. We asked for family pictures and family stories. The response was a treasure trove of stories about hard work and community spirit. We also began a systematic study of the Session Books kept by the elders who led the church through good times and bad. Both of these research paths convinced me of the importance of this church to all the people associated with it, past and present. I wanted to tell their stories.

And so I acknowledge the invaluable assistance of my good friends, Janice, Virginia, and the people of Meadow Creek. I acknowledge the important work done in 1987 by Rev. and Mrs. Richter, Helen and Jerry Neas, Ann Birdwell, Nancy Renner, Louann Southerland, and Barbara Thompson. I appreciate the editing work done by Erin Bellomy and the photography of

Letitia Ebmeyer. My husband, David, provided invaluable help preparing the pictures for publication.

My goal was to tell the stories of ordinary people possessed of a strong faith who have been blessed by God. While working on the cemetery project and this history, I was shaded by the magnificent oak tree in the churchyard. For me, it came to symbolize strength and stability, two character traits found in the members of my church home ...... *Ruth Kross*

Introduction

Meadow Creek Presbyterian Church in Greeneville, Tennessee, is just a small country church located in the southern part of Greene County near the Nolichucky River. It is a church with a 200 year history from pioneer days to the present. This book was written to tell the story of this congregation, not because it was so exceptional, but because it is the story of a people who believed God's covenant promises and who have recognized His providential care for 200 years.

The first meeting house was built in 1812 near the river. The cemetery was begun as a final resting place for the pioneering Cochran family and in the 1840s, when the Cochrans donated their land to the church, a new sanctuary was built near the cemetery. There are several unmarked graves here as well as the graves of the pioneering Cochrans, Greggs, Woods, and Hales. Each tombstone memorializes the life of a Christian who loved and was loved. Many elders and deacons lie here. Many remarkable Christian women are buried here. And thirty-six babies are buried here. Families rest together in death as they worked together in life.

Presbyterians believe that people are sinful, but God forgives because Jesus gained salvation and freedom for those who believe in Him. Consequently, it is their belief that saved sinners should live their lives in such a way as to bring glory to God. The church's founders were "Covenanters," people who believed that God's covenant as expressed to Abraham in Genesis 17:7 remained operative throughout time: *"And I will establish my covenant between me and you and your descendants after you throughout their generations for an everlasting covenant, to be God to you and to your descendants after you."*

Most history books describe great events or influential leaders who made a significant impact on the course of history. This little history book is different. The people in these stories are not influential. The events of their lives are not significant beyond their immediate families. However, the ordinariness of their lives is something most readers can relate to.

This book was written to glorify God for his continued providence over this small congregation. This is the story of faithful people who served God within their church and their community in gratitude for their salvation. They have always considered themselves as forgiven, in spite of their human frailties and faults, which they freely admit.

Meadow Creek Presbyterian Church has been, and strives to be a place with a historical faith for a new generation.

Chapter One

Planting the Seed

America's First Frontier . . .
Over the Mountains

The great oak tree in the churchyard began its life as a tiny acorn in the great forest that covered the "Overmountain" region of East Tennessee. It was a hilly and rock-strewn land of old growth forest containing massive chestnut trees, majestic oaks, poplars, elms, maples, and pines. It was home to herds of deer, elk, and even buffalo. Besides receiving abundant rainfall, the land was filled with natural springs, meandering creeks, and the fast-flowing Nolichucky River. Along the river, there were many areas of fertile bottom land.

This bottom land has provided a good place for people to live. Archaeologists from the University of Tennessee have unearthed evidence of thousands of years of human habitation along the river. At the time of America's founding, Native American tribes considered this land to be open to all for hunting. Cherokee from the east, Shawnee from the north, Chickasaw from the west, and Creeks from the south followed the rivers to these forests in order to hunt. These tribal hunters made few claims on the land other than the freedom to come, hunt, and go back to their villages.

To the British colonists living along the Atlantic seaboard, the Overmountain Region was the "First Frontier." Before there was a United States, long hunters, such as Daniel Boone, followed the great rivers and Indian trails of the region, pursuing game and furs. These long hunters were disobeying King George and the Proclamation of 1763 by crossing the ridge of the Appalachians, and they found an area ripe for settlement. A few hardy settlers, in defiance to the king, did come and build a few homesteads along the rivers.

Meadow Creek

The Nolichucky River lay at the southern end of the Great Valley, which stretched northward all the way to northern Virginia. It was through this valley that the first settlers came. In 1771, a man named Jacob Brown came to the Nolichucky River and leased thousands of acres from the Cherokee. His goal was to farm the land and trade with the Cherokee. With the Cherokee as landlords and the settlers as leaseholders, peaceful relations existed. On March 25, 1775, Jacob Brown purchased his leasehold from the Cherokee and proceeded to subdivide it and sell it to more settlers. Most of those early settlers were not English but Scotch-Irish, and therefore they did not have a high regard for the king.

The Overmountain Region was under the jurisdiction of the colony of North Carolina, although its distance from the state capital at Raleigh meant that the people along the Nolichucky were essentially on their own. So they formed the Wautauga Association and elected their own judges and militia leaders. This form of self-government preceded the independence movement of the original thirteen English colonies.

Throughout the 1700s, many Scotch-Irish Presbyterians left their homeland in Ulster, Ireland, crossed the Atlantic, and walked down the Great Valley from Pennsylvania to this Overmountain Region. Between 1771 and 1775, great waves of migrants came to the region because of religious persecution, famine, and political oppression in Ireland, and because of appeals from relatives already in the colonies. They may have left behind politically harsh conditions created by their rulers in Ireland, but the Overmountain Region presented them with other physically harsh conditions. Before they could farm the land, they had to cut down massive trees in the endless forests.

Soon, political events beyond their control would threaten these frontier settlements. They were the rear guard of the Colonial Rebellion against the English king and Parliament they had never liked anyway. When the Declaration of Independence was signed in 1776 and the Revolutionary War began, the English persuaded the Creeks, Cherokees, and Chickasaw to ally with them. The English promised guns, ammunition, and other trade goods if these tribal groups attacked the settlers. The western front of the Revolutionary War ran through the Overmountain Region.

This frontier war was brutal. Many settlers saw their homes and fields destroyed, but they fought back just as hard and just as brutally. Total war between the settlers and the Cherokee—in which both sides saw women, children, livestock, and crops as targets—continued sporadically from 1777 until it was ended by treaty in 1795, long after the Revolutionary War had ended. In spite of these dangerous years of conflict, settlers continued to make their way into the Nolichucky River area.

These frontier soldiers got involved in larger war in 1779, when the regular British army moved south to attack the Carolinas. Charleston quickly fell to the British, and Cornwallis's forces started moving inland and upland. As they did so, Scottish Col. Ferguson sent a written warning to the Overmountain settlements of Scotch-Irish immigrants telling them that he was coming to finish them off. In response to that warning, they mustered at Sycamore Shoals in order to launch a preemptive attack against Col. Ferguson. They brought their wives and children to Fort Wautauga. Before they marched, they listened to a sermon by the great Presbyterian preacher Rev. Samuel Doak, who compared them to Gideon's men. Rev. Doak prayed for their safety and success. The Overmountain Men brought their own ammunition and supplies, traveled for two weeks, fought for two hours, and wiped out Ferguson and his men at the battle of King's Mountain in October of 1780. General Nathanael Greene credited this battle with turning the tide of the Revolutionary War in the South in favor of the Americans.

One year later, in October of 1781, George Washington defeated Cornwallis at Yorktown and the United States gained its independence from England. Many cash-strapped colonies paid their soldiers with land grants in the western lands. North Carolina paid its soldiers with land grants in the Overmountain Region, which had by then been named the Southwest Territory. Most of the land not owned by Jacob Brown was granted to Gen. Nathanael Greene, Washington's trusted general. He died shortly after the war, and his land was sold off. Mr. Robert Kerr purchased some of that land and founded a town named Greeneville in 1783. North Carolina ceded jurisdiction of the territory to the Federal government in 1788, and Tennessee became the sixteenth state in 1796.

Greene County was named for General Nathanael Greene. Greeneville became the county seat, and a courthouse was built near the Presbyterian church. Davy Crockett was born along the Nolichucky River in Greene County in 1786, and President Andrew Johnson arrived in Greeneville in 1826. Besides the Scotch-Irish Presbyterians, German Lutherans and Pennsylvania Quakers also moved into the area when the Revolutionary War ended. The 1790 Census listed a total population of 7,741, of whom 454 were slaves. Approximately 70,000 people call Greene County home today. It remains the largest agricultural county in Tennessee.

It was within this historical context that the founders of Meadow Creek Presbyterian Church moved onto the lands along the Nolichucky River. They were either the offspring of Revolutionary War veterans or they bought land from veterans who needed cash.

The Meadow Creek community was a day's journey by horseback from Greeneville, a journey that takes fifteen minutes today. There were two Presbyterian churches in town. The other Presbyterian church in Greene County, Timber Ridge, was much closer but was still at least an hour and a half away by horseback. Between the Meadow Creek community and those churches was the tumultuous Nolichucky River. For this reason, sons of Revolutionary War veterans organized the church in 1812.

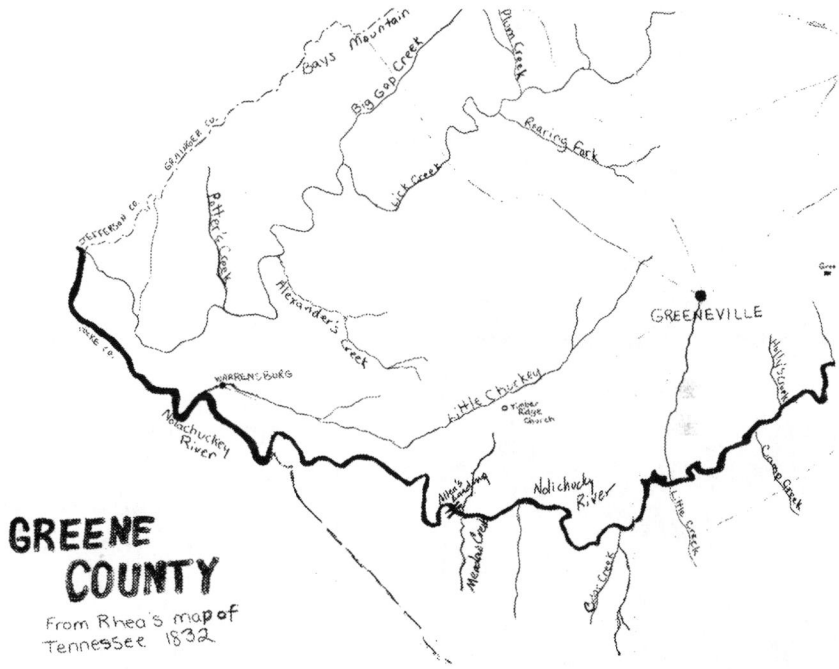

GREENE
COUNTY
From Rhea's map of
Tennessee 1832

This hand-drawn map of the area was first printed in the history of the Timber Ridge Presbyterian Church. While it shows the many creeks that make up the watershed of the Nolichucky River, it doesn't show how hilly and rocky the landscape is. The best agricultural land in the county is located along the river.

The Germination of Meadow Creek

Bottom land along the Nolichucky was some of the most fertile land in eastern Tennessee. Upland from the river, the soil was mostly clay, but it was suitable for corn and, in later years, burley tobacco. It was a great place to raise livestock, especially pigs.

Michael Woods obtained land near the Nolichucky River. He named the small creek on his property Meadow Creek. Michael Woods was a visionary pioneer, and he saw the opportunity to create a settlement complete with a mill and a schoolhouse.

Like all the pioneers, Michael Woods faced the daunting task of felling huge trees in order to open up farmland and to build his home, mill, and school. The schoolhouse he built was a two-story log cabin, and he named it the Meadow Creek Academy. Mr. Woods was a devout Presbyterian, and by 1812, he had encouraged his neighbors—the Greggs, Cochrans, Crawfords, and others—to attend Presbyterian worship services at the academy whenever the services of a minister could be obtained. Mr. Woods was an elder at the Timber Ridge Presbyterian Church.

Timber Ridge had been organized in 1787 on the other side of the Nolichucky River by the frontier pastor Rev. James Balch, who was assisted by Rev. Samuel Doak. By 1797, it was the church home of thirty frontier families. By 1800, Rev. James Witherspoon (grandson of Dr. John Witherspoon, president of Princeton College and signer of the Declaration of Independence) led a series of Camp Meetings and shepherded more growth for the Timber Ridge congregation. When Rev. Witherspoon left in 1805, the congregation was unable to secure another pastor, and the pulpit remained vacant until 1818.

It was because of the long journey, hazardous river crossing, and "unsettled" conditions at Timber Ridge that two of its elders, Michael Woods and John Gregg, began organizing services at Meadow Creek Academy in 1812.

The little congregation of Meadow Creek continued to hold services as often as possible in the academy building. They had to rely on circuit-riding ministers who tended to spiritual needs of the pioneers in exchange for a bed and food. Since there were some Presbyterian ministers in Greene County, it can be assumed that they met frequently, although there are no written records to substantiate this.

George Cochran lived downriver from Michael Woods, and his sons probably learned to read and write at Meadow Creek Academy. By 1812, he took them to preaching services at the academy. The Cochran's had extensive land holdings along the river. They built a home near a spring that fed into the river, and on a hilltop overlooking his homestead, an acorn had sprouted. It sent down a strong tap root, and grew into a sturdy sapling oak.

Presbyterianism in East Tennessee

1798—Rev. S. Doak and Rev. H. Balch take opposite sides in the Hopkinsian controversy. Presbyterianism in Greene County is divided by loyalties to either of these great preachers. The "New Divinity" faction (Hopkinsians) leaves Mount Bethel and forms Harmony Presbyterian Church.

1800 - Sinking Springs changes its location and name to Timber Ridge Presbyterian Church.

1812—Under the leadership of Michael Woods and John Gregg, elders of both Harmony and Timber Ridge Churches, the Meadow Creek Congregation begins holding services.

1837—Meadow Creek Presbyterian Church is organized with twenty-six members, in the French Broad Presbytery. Rev. Nathaniel Hood presided over the first service, held on June 3, 1837. Rev. Samuel Gregg, son of John Gregg, served as the first pastor, 1837-1843.

These early Christians, the Greggs, Cochrans, Woods, and others, who lived close to the Nolichucky formed the sturdy trunk of the Presbyterian family tree that sprouted at Meadow Creek. Like the red oak on the Cochran land, that church grew from its Calvinistic taproot for the next 200 years.

Presbyterianism in East Tennessee

The frontier churches endured three theological controversies in the first half of the 19th century:

Hopkinsian *was introduced by Rev. H. Balch and disputed by Rev. S. Doak and the controversy ruined their friendship. The controversy led to the "unsettled" conditions at Timber Ridge. The dispute arose out of the teachings of the famous preacher, Jonathan Edwards. It had to do with God's sovereignty and the nature of sin. (1808-1815)*

New School/Old School Controversy *centered around missionary activities and union with the Congregational denominations of New England. Most of the eleven Presbyterian churches in East Tennessee favored the union. The emphasis on new mission activities put them solidly in the New School faction. (1830s)*

The Cumberland Split *occurred because of the fervency of the Great Awakening on the frontier. Churches in Kentucky and Tennessee that were created after revival meetings couldn't wait for preachers educated and licensed by the General Assembly of the Presbyterian Church. By removing that requirement, they created a new Presbyterian denomination. (1840s)*

Presbyterianism in the early 1800s followed the teachings of John Calvin of the Reformation and his fellow reformer, John Knox of Scotland. Calvin emphasized the need for individual believers to study Scripture, so Christians had to know how to read. Calvin taught the importance of a believer's faith in God, His grace and His providence. Calvin believed that man's gratitude for his salvation required people to do all things to the glory of God. In other words, good works were not required *for* salvation but in grateful response *to* salvation.

John Calvin also described a Christian's relationship to God as a "covenantal relationship." Believers are faithful because God is faithful. God has granted forgiveness for all sins; therefore man lives as righteously as possible to bring honor and glory to God. Families must teach these truths to each new generation, thus Calvinists stressed the need to educate each generation of believers. In fact, education is second only to public worship in importance to Presbyterians. That is why the log cabin built at Meadow Creek served as both a church and school. That is why classical scholars with PhD's in theology from Princeton University traveled by horseback throughout the frontier to preach to these pioneers.

For twenty-five years, a small group of Presbyterians sent their sons to the academy and met sporadically for worship on Sunday. By 1837, the congregation felt sufficiently strong in numbers and finances to organize as a church in the French Broad Presbytery. Meadow Creek Congregation has met as a fellowship of believers since 1812 and as an organized church since 1837. Therefore, some people would say the church is 175 years old, but most people consider it be 200 years old.

The information in the text boxes concerning the Time-Line and the Controversies was obtained from an article, "Annals of Timber Ridge Church," by Harry Roberts. This article appeared on pages 1-24 in the book, *Timber Ridge Church: A 200 Year Heritage of Presbyterian Faith, 1786-1986.* Mr. Roberts did extensive research in "The Minutes of Hanover Presbytery," "Session Books of Timber Ridge," *The Presbyterian Church Throughout the World,* (1874), "Minutes of Abingdon Presbytery," and *A Historical Sketch of the Synod of Tennessee,* (Alexander).

Because elders Michael Woods and John Gregg of Meadow Creek were elders in Timber Ridge, and the Cochrans were members of Timber Ridge, they were probably familiar with the controversies. In an era before radio, television, movies, and sports, discussion of theological issues was second only to political debates as topics of conversation.

Also, the Hopkinsian Controversy destroyed the relationship between Rev. Samuel Doak, "The Apostle of Religion and Learning" and Rev. Hezekiah Balch. Both men founded churches and academies in Greeneville, but if they happened to meet on Main Street, they walked on opposite sides of the street. Descendants of these pioneer preachers met for a joint worship service at the Big Spring in downtown Greeneville in 2004 and declared their relationship "restored."

Pioneer Life and Worship

Volumes have been written about the difficulties and hardships faced by the pioneers who settled the frontier. However, because they knew no other way of life, the pioneers would not have described their lives as difficult or hard. They took pride in their independence and self-sufficiency; the daily toil of farming the land and tending the livestock was exactly what they wanted to do. It was hard work, but they were working for themselves.

This is a photograph of a surviving two-story log building with a stone chimney. It is not a photograph of Meadow Creek Academy, but it can be assumed that the building looked very similar to this as there was not much variety in log cabin construction.

If they couldn't make what they needed, or trade for what they needed, they did without and did not complain. Every spring, they worked the soil and planted corn, flax, vegetables, and herbs.

Even today planting seeds is an act of faith. So many hazards can prevent a good harvest. Farmers must fight the ravenous birds, destructive raccoons, and a myriad of harmful insects. Drought and flood can destroy a year's food supply.

Whatever was harvested in the fall had to last a year. Beans, fruits, and herbs were dried. Meat was smoked and salted. Flax and wool were processed, spun, woven, and sewn. The pioneers who worked the land had faith that God would bless their efforts and provide their harvest, because they knew that so many things were outside of their control.

The most daunting hardship on the frontier was the lack of medical care. Medicinal herbs and corn liquor were the only palliatives available. Complications of childbirth were often fatal to both mother and infant. Because so much was beyond their control, each pioneer understood that their lives, and the lives of their children, were simply in God's hands. Because death was a frequent visitor, believers could take comfort that the joys and sorrows were all part of God's will, His providence.

The pioneer settlers worshipping at Meadow Creek had a deep faith in their God. As their numbers grew, they decided that they were ready to become independent of Timber Ridge Church. They followed proper Presbyterian procedures, elected officers and asked the Lord's blessings on their future plans.

The first entry in the first book of Session Minutes records:

> *"On March 25, 1837, it was resolved by a meeting of some of the members of Timber Ridge Church, at Meadow Creek Academy to petition French Broad Presbytery to set off those members of Timber Ridge Church who live on the south side of Nola Chuck (sic) and organize them into a separate church. The petition was laid before Presbytery at their meeting at Greeneville on April, 1837. Presbytery granted the request, and appointed Rev. Nathaniel Hood to attend to the business."*

On June 3, 1837, Rev. Hood met the congregation at Meadow Creek Academy and constituted twenty six members into a church. On the same day, the church elected as its first elders John Gregg, James Dunlap, Jacob Kelly, and Samuel Cochran.

The first roll of Meadow Creek contained twenty-four named individuals who came from several families:

> John and Hannah Gregg with daughter Susan Gregg, and daughter-in-law Alpha Shields married to son, Marshall who would join in 1838.
> Michael and Esther Woods
> John and Caroline Cochran Dunlap with daughters, Margaret and Jane
> John and Jane Jordan
> Samuel and Mary Cochran
> John, Nancy, and Katherine Reynolds
> Jacob and Ann Kelley
> James Thompson
> Jane Cook
> Isabella Buster
> Mary Masenor
> Margaret Allen Crawford
> Three "colored" persons named William, Peter, and Sarah Crawford were also entered into membership.

Besides the academy building, which served as both school and church, the most important building in the Meadow Creek community was the mill, also built by Michael Woods. Farther downriver, John Gregg and his son, Marshall, built a mill on a creek that flowed into the Nolichucky River. Gregg's Mill served the Caney Branch Community. The Greggs ground the corn of their neighbors so that they could store their corn meal in clay crocks. The path to this mill became known as Gregg Mill Road.

Margaret Crawford and her family were neighbors of Michael and Esther Wood, and they farmed the rich bottom land along the river. The Crawford's land along the Nolichucky was a great place to ford the river and head toward Greeneville or to Timber Ridge. When Margaret's husband, William, died, her brother, James Allen, paid the taxes and bought the land. He improved the land and created a safe place to ford the river. It was known as "Allen's Crossing." Eventually, his son, James Allen, Jr., built a bridge at the site. The path to his bridge became known as Allens Bridge Road.

Both Gregg Mill Road and Allens Bridge Road passed through land owned by Samuel Cochran. On a hill near the intersection of these roads, Samuel Cochran started a family cemetery at the base of a young oak tree. There were no headstones, just "tomb rocks." Sometime in the 1840s, Elder Gregg and Elder Cochran convinced Elder Wood that the Presbyterian congregation known as Meadow Creek should relocate to this Cochran land. His hilltop cemetery, at the intersection of Gregg Mill Road and Allens Bridge Road would be a more central location for the congregation.

An agreement was reached, a simple church was built, and the congregation worshipped regularly. Elder Gregg's son, Samuel Gregg, served as pastor from 1837-1843. He was a graduate of Tusculum College, the oldest college west of the mountains and a Presbyterian school founded by the son of Rev. Samuel Doak. In 1847, Dr. Francis McCorkle, another student of Rev. Doak, served Meadow Creek after pastoring at Mount Bethel in Greeneville and the Timber Ridge church.

Worship services consisted of singing, prayer, Bible reading, and sermons. Musical accompaniment, if there was any, probably came from a fiddle. The sermons were one to two hours long. Because the congregants often traveled for at least an hour, they brought their mid-day meal with them and had "dinner on the grounds." Sunday School and various meetings would then take place in the afternoon, after which everyone traveled back home. These early church members used the better part of the day to worship the Lord and fellowship with each other.

Much of the music of the early 1800s remains alive in East Tennessee in the Shape-Note Singing Schools that meet on a regular basis. In the *New Harp of Columbia Hymnbook* of 1848 there is a hymn that could have been used by the Meadow Creek congregation as they met in the new sanctuary at the new location:

Here, in thy name, eternal God,
We build this earthly house for thee;
Oh, choose it for thy fix'd abode,
And guard it long from error free!

Here, when thy people seek thy face,
And dying sinners pray to live;
Hear thou, in heaven, thy dwelling place,
And when thou hearest, Lord, forgive.

Here, when thy messengers proclaim
The blessed gospel of thy Son,
Still by the power of his great name
Be signs and wonders done.

Thy glory never hence depart,
Yet choose not, Lord, this house alone;
Thy kingdom come to every heart
In every bosom fix thy throne.

Descendants of Michael Woods

There are no photographs of Michael and Esther Woods, but their son, David Leonias Woods followed in his father's footsteps and provided leadership to Meadow Creek for many years as an Elder and Clerk of the Session. This is his family:

Back: *Eliza Woods, *Willie Hugh Woods, Bess Woods Noel, *Scott Cloyd Woods, *Belle Wagner Woods, *Florence Woods Mitchell.
Front: *Samuel Shields Woods, *Charlie B. Woods, Knox Woods (infant), *David Leonidas Woods, Montie Wagner, Belle Wagner Woods, *Madge Mitchell Davis.
Seated: David Cloyd.
*These members are at rest under the Tree in the Churchyard.

Covenanters: The Roots of Meadow Creek

Genesis 17:7, *"And I will establish my covenant between me and you and your descendants after you throughout their generations for an everlasting covenant, to be God to you and to your descendants after you."*

"Besides this, he not only testified that he was, but also promised that he would ever be, their God. This he did that their hope, not content with present benefits, might be extended to eternity. Many passages show that this characterization of the future life was so understood among them, when believers were comforted not only amid present misfortunes but for the future by the thought that God would never fail them . . . . God, however, whose beneficence is not hindered by death, does not withdraw the fruit of his mercy from the dead, but for their sake 'conveys it to a thousand generations.'"
(John Calvin, *Institutes of the Christian Religion*, II.X.9)

John Calvin wrote the *Institutes* in 17th century Switzerland and his teachings had a great impact on John Knox, the founder of the Scottish Presbyterian Church. Understanding that salvation comes by faith alone and that faith comes from knowledge of God's word, Presbyterianism promotes strong families and Christian education. The children of believers must be educated in the faith so that they claim their heritage and pass it on.

In contrast to the "High-Church" tradition of the English, the Scotch-Irish Presbyterians were "Low-Church." The high and low distinction refers to the forms of church government. The Anglican and Episcopal churches are governed by a hierarchy of officials. Power comes from the top down. In Presbyterian churches, leadership comes from the bottom up. Congregations elect elders who attend Presbyteries, or regional gatherings, and denominational decisions are made at national General Assemblies. Meadow Creek was founded by experienced elders, Michael Woods and John Gregg. When Samuel Cochran joined the church in 1837, he too became an elder and held this leadership post for over fifty years. Because of the lay-leadership of these men, Meadow Creek Presbyterian Church held together throughout the nineteenth Century despite sporadic pastoral care, financial difficulties, denominational conflicts within the larger Presbyterian Assemblies, and Civil War.

An analysis of the family trees of these men illustrates how God's covenantal promises provided for Meadow Creek. Michael Woods built Meadow Creek Academy and organized the first worship services. His grandson, David Leonidas Woods, served as elder from 1878 until his death in 1932. There are nine Woods family members buried under the great oak tree.

John Gregg moved to Greene County as a child in 1788. He grew up in the first brick home in Greene County. He built a mill and organized two churches. His son, Marshall (1807-1894) joined Meadow Creek Church in 1838, became an elder in 1844, and served in that leadership capacity for over fifty years. His other son, Samuel was a Presbyterian minister and served at Meadow Creek from 1837-1843. His grandson, Nathaniel Chambers, also served as elder and provided leadership during the construction of the current sanctuary. Many of John Gregg's descendants are also resting in the cemetery of Meadow Creek.

Samuel Cochran moved to Greene County as a nine year old child in 1809. He was thirty-seven when Meadow Creek was organized and he became an elder, serving in that capacity for almost fifty years. His first wife, Mary Ann, died when he was forty-six. He married Eliza Hale, twenty years his junior, who gave birth to six more children in addition to the three children he already had. The son of Samuel and Eliza, James Alfred Cochran (1848-1934) served as deacon and Sunday School teacher. His grandson-in-law, James Anderson Kiser (1861-1923), served as an elder for thirty-one years. Another grandson-in-law, Charles J. Waddell (1878-1961), served as deacon, elder and song-leader. Charles Waddell and Bessie Mae Kiser Waddell were

> *Like Abraham of the Old Testament, the Rev. Samuel Doak exemplified the concept of Covenant. The great preacher and teacher started several churches and schools. During his 81 years, he taught two generations of teachers and preachers. And for nine generations, a Samuel Doak has been involved in the Presbyterian Church and supportive of Christian education, particularly Tusculum College.*

the progenitors of numerous Waddells, Crums, Neases, Raders, Kings, and Wilhoits who grew up in the church, learned their catechism in the church, and are buried in the churchyard under the big tree. In the current congregation, Charles Love, is a direct descendant of Samuel Cochran and he, too, has served as deacon and elder. Samuel Cochran lived out his faith and taught that faith to his children and grandchildren. God blessed Samuel Cochran and his descendants for seven generations.

These early Covenanters not only believed God's covenant promises for their families, but also sought to proclaim the gospel to their Meadow Creek Community in obedience to Christ's Great Commission. When the Presbyterian Church in the United States split into two factions, the New School and Old School in 1837, Meadow Creek joined the New School Holston Presbytery and supported its works of evangelism, church-planting, and missions. At special brush-arbor and camp meetings, the gospel was preached to the unchurched, and members were added to the congregation. This outreach saw major membership gains to the congregation in the late 1860s, 1880s, 1890s, 1914, and 1950s. In 1915, Meadow Creek planted the New Ebenezer church further south on Allens Bridge Road, and supported it until 1934, when it became self-sufficient.

Although today's Presbyterians no longer call themselves Covenanters, the concept has never left their church programs and policies. Sunday School begins for children at age three or four. Meadow Creek has financially supported foreign missions throughout the 20th Century. From the 1950s to the present, Meadow Creek has reached out to youth of the community through various activities such as Vacation Bible Schools, softball leagues, Pioneer Clubs, and the current Youth Group. Starting in 2008, Meadow Creek has reached out to the wider community through its Community Fun Day, and special programs.

Chapter Two

The Ways of the Lord . . . . His Providence

The Presbyterian belief in God's providence for His people comes from a careful reading of the Scriptures. The Old Testament book of Exodus explains how God provided manna for the Israelites every day they wandered in the wilderness. In the Sermon on the Mount, Jesus taught, *"Therefore do not be anxious about tomorrow, for tomorrow will be anxious for itself. Let the day's own trouble be sufficient for the day."* (Matt. 6:34) Scripture teaches that God will provide for His people. The good times are from Him.

But what about when times are bad? How does Providence fit into that? Why do bad things happen? Christians of all denominations have struggled to understand this reality. Why did Job suffer horrendous losses? Why were the early Christians persecuted? Why do babies die? For Presbyterians, the answer lies in understanding that God is omnipotent, or all-powerful, yet He allows wars, sickness, and untimely death to remind His people to trust in Him. Job understood that. He said, *"Shall we receive good at the hand of God, and shall we not receive evil?"* (Job 2:10) Human beings are sinful and they do hurt each other. Human beings are also capable of forgiveness and compassion, if their strength of character comes from knowing God.

For people unfamiliar with the teachings of Christianity, the concept of Providence is often difficult to understand. By focusing on a tragic **event** and asking, "Why did God allow that," they don't comprehend that God uses events to fit His **plan**. Studying the history of a Christian church over 200 years provides the long-term perspective necessary to understand why things happen the way they do. Meadow Creek's history has many examples of how God works through both good and bad **events** to bring His people closer to Him, which is His ultimate **plan**.

Meadow Creek Presbyterian Church was started in the wilderness at a time when day to day survival was the highest priority. God provided for His people. When the church was forty-nine years old, a great and destructive war overwhelmed the congregation. Despite many physical losses, God's people recovered and enjoyed great prosperity and increase. When confronted with great sin among its members, God provided grace. When tragedy struck a beloved pastor, God provided comfort. When theological disputes tore Presbyterianism apart, God guided Meadow Creek. When disputes with two different pastors almost destroyed the congregation, God provided renewal. And from the beginning, God provided the financial means to keep Meadow Creek free from debt. God worked through good times and bad times to bring His people closer to Him.

A lot happens over 200 years. But, as the apostle Paul learned over his tumultuous life, *"We know that in everything God works for good with those who love him, who are called according to his purpose."* Romans 8:28

The Great Unpleasantness . . . . Civilian Wars within the Civil War

With the coming of the 1850s, the small congregation at Meadow Creek had big issues to deal with. The leading Presbyterian ministers in Greene County, Rev. Samuel Doak and Rev. Hezekiah Balch were both anti-slavery. Since they were also the main teachers of new pastors, clerical opposition to slavery was very strong. But many Presbyterians owned between two and twenty slaves. Meadow Creek slave holders brought their slaves to church to worship regularly. They buried their slaves in the churchyard under the oak tree.

The slavery question would prove disastrous to not only Presbyterianism, but also the Baptists, Methodists, and the whole country. These mainline denominations split into northern and southern factions over the issue of slavery in the late 1850s, even before the nation split apart. Meadow Creek joined the United Synod of the Presbyterian Church, which believed that the issue of slavery was not desirable, but should not be made an issue in the church. The northern Presbyterian synods were abolitionists.

When the war came, it arrived with a vengeance in East Tennessee. When Tennessee became the last state to secede from the Union, the political leadership of East Tennessee attempted to secede from the state. The Greeneville Union Convention took a vote in 1861 to secede from Tennessee, because East Tennessee wanted to stay in the Union and not join the Confederacy. That vote resulted in having the governor send occupational troops to the area. Senator Andrew Johnson of Greeneville was the only southern Senator to remain in Washington although he had to leave occupied Greeneville. And President Lincoln wrote to General Buell, "My distress is that our friends in East Tennessee are being hanged and driven to despair." (Sandburg, p. 328)

While the Civil War tore the United States in two, and great armies met on various battlefields throughout the South, a four year period of virtual anarchy descended upon the civilian population of Greene County. Neighbor turned against neighbor. Many families watched one son fight for the Union and another for the Confederacy. Civilian government ceased. Schools closed. Churches stopped holding services. Travel was not safe. Citizens went into survival mode.

The "civil war" within the Civil War also affected Meadow Creek. John Fannon joined the Union Army and W. G. Broyles, William Cochran, James Yearwood, and William Kiser joined the Confederacy. There are no records of church meetings from August 19, 1862, until June 12, 1865. No baptisms were recorded. The study of Scripture and prayers took place in individual homes, not in the church sanctuary. The prayers for protection from enemies must have been fervently and frequently raised because enemies were everywhere. Before the war, they were brothers, neighbors, customers, and friends. Now they were Bushwackers, Home Guards, Conscripters, and Raiders.

Greene County changed hands about forty times during the course of the war. No major battles were fought, but skirmishes and ambushes between the two sides were a regular occurrence. The bands of roving Yankees and Rebels had to live off the land. Consequently, they terrorized the local farm families. When they skirmished and died, they were buried locally. Many such casualties are buried in the churchyard, without a record of their names or ranks. They lie under the oak tree in unmarked graves.

The Civil War tore the Meadow Creek community apart. Samuel Cochran's brother, George, a member of Timber Ridge, lost all of his sons to the conflict. They died in a prisoner of war camp outside of Chicago. He himself was killed by raiders who came to his farm and demanded his horses. He tried to fight them off, but they killed him.

The brother of Margaret Crawford, Old James Allen or "Devil Jim" as he was called, started a feud with the Seaton and Davis families who were his neighbors. Joe Davis was a tenant farmer on Michael Woods' farm. Joe's son, John Davis, and John's brother-in-law, William Seaton, joined the Confederate Army. That's what most of the young men in the community did. However, the Confederate Army couldn't pay its soldiers and both John Davis and William Seaton had young families. When they heard the Union Army not only paid its soldiers but promised them a pension, both men switched sides in July of 1863.

By August of 1864, they were back in East Tennessee with Company B, 8th Regiment of the Tennessee Cavalry (Union). And in December, they donned cast-off Confederate uniforms and tried to get home to their wives. James Allen heard they were around and roused up the Confederates in the area by claiming they were spies. John Davis and William Seaton were found and killed by a group led by William Seaton's cousin, Jesse Holt.

In revenge, Joe Davis found an opportunity to shoot James Allen while he was fording the Nolichucky River. His shotgun missed vital organs but put a real hurtin' on his backside.

Old James Allen, "Devil Jim," tried to make the most of the chaos all around him. He sold chickens, horses, and food stuffs to both sides. Better to make a buck than take a bullet. But the Confederate dollars were worthless after the war. He had also purchased Confederate Bonds in the hopes of supporting the war and making a gain. Instead, he lost all of these investments, had to sell off some of his prime land, and died heavily in debt. He also lost a lot of friends after the war because of his double-dealing.

Other civilian victims of these foraging soldiers developed different ways to survive.

The Crum family homeplace in Cedar Creek still has a Yankee bullet in the newel post of the staircase. In 1999, Launa Crum told the story of how the family hid their food from rampaging soldiers. When they heard that raiders were coming through, they put their smoked meat in bed with their elderly grandma. They had learned that both Yankees and Rebels had been raised to respect their elders, and therefore they would not harass the "sickbed" of grandma. The fifth commandment spared the hams and bacon.

The Russell sisters were very young during the war. Their job was to care for the family cow. They were able to protect the family milk supply by hiding the cow in a sinkhole. They remained spinsters all their lives, however, probably because about forty percent of Tennessee's young male population lost their lives in the war. There were not enough husbands to go around.

Despite these few examples of successful survival strategies, by 1865 the people of Greene County were in very dire straits. "Weeds had taken over fields, there were few seeds to plant, few tools with which to farm, and few horses, mules, cattle, hogs or sheep. Some fortunate families had relatives in the North who sent seed to them, others had to beg seeds from the government." (Bible, Mitzi) Most of the split-rail fences were gone, burned in the campfires of the raiders.

The wounds ran deep. Families were forever split apart. Friendships were destroyed. All the institutions of civilization so carefully nurtured during the rugged pioneer era had to be rebuilt: churches, schools, medical care, and markets. It would take another generation for the suffering to end.

Those that survived praised the Lord for their survival and prayed for His blessings on what was left of their families. They rebuilt fences and herds. They planted their seeds.

Once the small congregation of Meadow Creek reorganized in June of 1865, they counted the cost and carried on. In August of 1866, they held a series of camp meetings on the grounds, under the oak tree in the churchyard. They rededicated themselves to the Lord's work. As a result of sound preaching, many people started attending regular services. In 1867, Meadow Creek almost tripled the size of its membership when seventy-two people joined the church, including "Devil Jim," or Mr. James Allen. After all he and the others had experienced, the words of Ephesians 2: 8-9 had a powerful and personal meaning: *"For by grace you have been saved through faith; and this is not your own doing, it is the gift of God—not because of works, lest any man should boast."* With 100 communicant members, Meadow Creek was the largest it would ever be. And in the 1870s, the new and larger meeting house, the first brick church, was completed.

From 1869 till 1876, Meadow Creek enjoyed the ministries of George Aiken Calwell. He provided sound leadership and pastoral stability. For the first time in its history, Meadow Creek had a pastoral relationship that lasted more than three years. And the Lord blessed the membership with many new babies.

This photograph, taken in the 1890s was discovered without any identifications. It's plain to see that everyone is dressed in their Sunday best with many fine hats. It's also plain to see that they had many children in the congregation.

A Time of Troubles . . .
A Murder in the Family

"Have mercy on me, O God, according to thy steadfast love; according to thy abundant mercy blot out my transgressions."
Psalm 51:1

Beginning in 1900, the hard-working James Polk Doggett became the pastor of Meadow Creek. He was in his late forties, lived in Chuckey and preached in seven churches in Greene and Hamblen Counties. Because of this workload, Rev. Doggett could not preach every Sunday. To compensate for that, he would conduct week-long camp meetings during the summer months. These meetings were held at the end of the work day and worshippers would come for spirited preaching, joyous singing, fervent prayers, and revival. Another purpose of the meetings was to "bring in the sheep." In 1906, Rev. Doggett baptized the family of W. A. and Sophina Bryant Houston. Their children, Kate, Perl, Salem, Rankin, Herman, and Nellie all made profession of faith in December of 1911 and became communicant members of Meadow Creek. Sometime between 1906 and 1911, W. A. Houston became a Trustee and also served on the Deacon Board.

By August of 1914, Meadow Creek was again without a pastor as Rev. Ambrose Wood left for Florida. Sadly, there was no pastor available when the Houston family suffered its first of two great losses. On October 31st, Sophina Houston died. Her youngest child, Nellie, was only sixteen. By the time the month of November ended, the family would suffer a tragedy of Shakespearean proportions.

Nellie had become pregnant by her cousin, Issac Houston, who promptly planned to marry her. Accompanied by his friend, Mr. Sexton, and with the proper marriage license in hand, Issac Houston came to his uncle's home to pick up his young bride. As the two young men approached the house, they met Rankin Houston who was armed. Rankin said, "Ike, it is too bad that this trouble has gotten up."

When they got to the front steps, Rankin said again, "Ike, it is a shame that you have wronged my sister and trampled the family underfoot." Issac Houston bent down to tend to his shoes and put his hand in his left pocket. At that point, Rankin fired two shots into Issac and killed him instantly. There would be no wedding that day.

The Greene County Sheriff was called. Rankin was arrested, and W. A. Houston was also taken into custody. Both father and son were charged. The jury found them guilty of murder in the first degree with mitigating circumstances. They were sentenced to life in prison.

Within nine months, sixteen year old Nellie Houston lost her mother, watched her brother kill her fiancé, testified at the trial of her brother and father, saw them off to prison, and gave birth to a beautiful baby girl she named Irene. Who helped her deal with all her troubles? Who gave her the strength to carry on?

The elders of Meadow Creek were confronted with a murder in one of the families of the church, and an unwed, pregnant teenager. One of its deacons, and a trustee of the church, was convicted of the crime along with his son. How did they administer justice and mercy? The Session book says nothing about how they handled the incident.

The shooting took place on November 18, 1914. W. A. Houston and his son, Rankin, were convicted on March 15, 1915. The only mention of the Houstons occurred on September 12, 1915, when "The resignation of Mr. W. A. Houston as trustee of Meadow Creek church was accepted." The membership list for W. A. Houston and Rankin Houston simply says, "Absent," and for Nellie, a simple "?". From her obituary, we know that Nellie moved to town and remained a Presbyterian her whole life.

Perhaps the silence of the elders on the incident indicated their belief that what happened was between the Houston family and God. Perhaps they understood from their study of Scripture that even biblical heroes like David had serious family problems. Perhaps they remembered the admonition of Jesus to the Pharisees, "Let him who is without sin among you be the first to throw a stone at her." (John 8:3)

Perhaps their silence is a lesson. Maybe when bad things happen to people it is best to "Be still and know that I am God."

What we do know about Meadow Creek in 1915 is that they had to prepare a yearly report to Presbytery about the condition of the church as a whole. Every church had to fill out a standardized evaluation form that covered the following issues:

1. Report on statistics and systematic beneficence.
2. A narrative on the programs and progress of the church.

The report for 1915 was carefully and thoroughly prepared. There were seventy-five "resident communicants" and twenty-one on the "cradle roll." The pastor's salary was $270.00. Summarizing the church year they wrote:

> The attendance upon the service of the sanctuary by members and by others is very good. About one-fourth of the heads of families observe family worship. The observance of the Lord's Day by members is very good. The children are trained in the Sabbath School in the catechism, but we fear they are neglected in the home. Our people are very faithful in worshiping the Lord with their substance. Our pastor's salary is always paid fully and promptly. There has been no manifestation of the Holy Spirit's power in our church. Worldly conformity does not exist, only to a small degree. There is some evangelistic work being done outside of our bounds. There are no special efforts made to secure recruits to the gospel ministry.
> (Session Book)

Because this report was due every year, it helped to focus pastors and elders on programs of education and benevolence. The spiritual health of the church was evaluated based on its progress, lack of worldliness, evangelism, and raising up new, young leadership. There was no question on the annual evaluation which required the description of a murder, criminal trial, and the life-imprisonment of a deacon and trustee.

Neither the report to Presbytery nor the Session Minutes described how God was at work within the Houston family and the Meadow Creek family. All of the people involved just kept on doing their daily work, attended weekly worship services, and prayed. The tragic events of 1914-1916 involving the Houston family did not rend the Meadow Creek family.

God was with Nellie. In 1917, Nellie suffered one more tragic loss when her older sister Pearl died after giving birth to twins. Shortly thereafter, Nellie married her sister's husband and raised her sister's children. All three children lived in a home with a mother and a father. Nellie's life had a new purpose and three innocent children grew up in a Christian home. She and her husband had been married for fifty years when he died in 1967. She lived as a widow for another sixteen years. Nellie died in April of 1983 at the age of 84. She was a faithful member of the Cumberland Presbyterian Church.

Tomorrow Still Comes

In 1960, Rev. John Powers accepted a call to Meadow Creek after serving for ten years at Cedar Creek Presbyterian Church and Mt. Zion Presbyterian Church. Rev. Powers felt called to the ministry to do three things at every church in which he served. First, he wanted to build up the church membership numerically and spiritually. Second, he wanted to build up the community through sports leagues, group fellowships, and economic opportunity. Third, he wanted to build up the fellowship within the church. At Mt. Zion Church, he also re-built the church building from the basement to the sanctuary. Throughout the reconstruction, he built up the fellowship of Mt. Zion through numerous work parties consisting of both youth workers from the denomination and craftsmen from the congregation. The membership addressed him as "architect, draftsman, construction foreman, carpenter, and minister." (Greeneville Sun, 1952)

John and Esther Powers circa 1960

Rev. Powers came to Greene County from Zenia, Ohio. When he got here, his mentor, Dr. Boyer, told him to invest in some practical tools so that he could help his neighbors and "get on the same plane" as they. Rev. Powers understood what it meant to be a shepherd and never saw the role of the pastor as being an administrator removed from the day-to-day realities of life. Consequently, his daughter, Janice Hoyle, remembers being afraid of tobacco harvesting time. If her dad saw someone at work in the fields, he made the family get out of the car and help out. Tobacco harvesting is very hard work, and Janice didn't like it.

When he came to Meadow Creek in 1960, Rev. Powers continued his three-point program of building up the church, the community, and the fellowship of the congregation. He built a softball field and organized community softball teams for men and women. He organized all-day molasses makings, and a traveling choir. Remembering the ministry of Rev. Powers, members said of him: "He made everybody feel like family;" "It was a joyful time;" and "He was a good teacher of the Bible."

But shortly after coming to Meadow Creek, in August of 1960, his wife Esther was diagnosed with colon cancer. She died prematurely at the age of 43 in April of 1961. Rev. Powers and his family had to deal with the loss of a valuable partner in his ministry and the mother of his six children. Esther Powers had actively shared in her husband's three-point program. She taught classes for the Red Cross Home Nursing Program. She made clothes for her own family as well as other people in the community. She made Christmas gifts for all the women in the church. She cooked for anybody suffering from sickness in the family.

She died in Laughlin Hospital and the people of Meadow Creek had already stepped up to care for her children. The youngest, George, age four, had been taken in by Rusty and Tine Miller, who became his second family. Young Margie, aged fifteen, had to assume many of the chores of her mother. The whole South Greene Community showered the grieving family with love and support. As the Greeneville Sun recorded:

> *George Powers tells the story of how Rev. Powers had to deal with new issues after Esther died. She had ruled the family with an "iron-clad" hand. Now, Rev. Powers had to assume all the discipline.*
>
> *One Sunday, George, Paul, and Johnny were fooling around in the back row of church during the morning service. Rev. Powers announced an unscheduled hymn, "Love Lifted Me," and asked the congregation to sing all four verses.*
>
> *He left the pulpit, took his three sons out to the porch and "wore us out."*
>
> *George now sings the song as "Love Whip-ped me."*

Hundreds of Greene Countians mourned the passing of Mrs. John E. Powers as was evidenced by the tremendous crowd that gathered at Kiser Funeral Home Sunday to pay their last respects to the 43 year old cancer victim.

By 12:30 pm, with the funeral some two hours off, people were literally streaming by the dozens into the funeral parlor. By 2:30 every available seat was taken with hardly standing room only left. The route to Greene Lawn

Memory Gardens, Asheville Highway, where the body was interred, was thick with carloads of people who did not attend the services, backed into almost every roadside parking place waiting for the cortege to pass. (April, 1961)

Charles Birdwell created a memorial fund for Esther Powers. Donations were used to purchase a new organ for the church. Dedicated in 1962, the organ is still in use today.

From April of 1961 till November of 1963, Rev. Powers and family were challenged by their grief to say as Job did, *"The Lord gave, and the Lord has taken away; blessed be the name of the Lord."* (1:21) He often told his children, "Tomorrow still comes whether you want it to or not. You can wallow in self-pity, or you can look around and see at least three people who are worse off than you." His children had a very difficult time understanding why their mom was gone. But day by day, Rev. Powers exemplified how a life of faith, prayer, and service could alleviate grief. He and his family suffered privately while the congregation and community were thriving.

Then, in November of 1963, tragedy struck again.

The Powers family kept two fuel cans, one for kerosene and one for gasoline. Everybody in the family knew which was which. But an unwitting neighbor put gasoline in the kerosene can. On November 8, 1963, the family was preparing for Janice's birthday. Rev. Powers, Janice, and Paul picked up Margie from East Tennessee State University to bake Janice's cake and be there for her party. George had gone to the Millers after school to hang out until supper time. Johnny was at the neighbor's. It was a cool night, so Rev. Powers started a fire in the fire place. Twelve-year old Paul was helping his dad, and Janice was watching them both. Margie was on the phone with one of her friends. Rev. Powers picked up the fuel can that had always contained kerosene, but now, unknown to all of them, contained gasoline. Instead of boosting the fire, the gasoline exploded and flames engulfed Rev. Powers, Janice and young Paul. Margie saw the whole thing and screamed into the phone. Her quick-thinking friend immediately called for help. Margie tried to stomp out the flames on Janice. Rev. Powers grabbed Paul and rushed outside to drop and roll on the ground.

Johnny heard the commotion and came running home. He grabbed his blue corduroy FFA jacket, wrapped it around his father, and tried to smother the flames. Paul was sitting under a water spigot trying to douse the flames on his legs.

Instead of having a birthday party, Janice, Paul, and Rev. Powers were rushed to the hospital all suffering from first and second-degree burns on their lower torsos. Rev. Powers went into shock and was in and out of consciousness. Janice and Paul shared a hospital room where their oldest sister, Mickey, who was a nurse at the hospital, did her best to care for them. As the night wore on, Janice called for help for twelve year old Paul, whose breathing became more and more labored. Finally, Mickey and the other nurses removed Janice from the room because young Paul was dying.

By morning, Paul was dead because, in addition to the burns on his legs, his lungs had been scorched by the flames. Janice was in serious condition, and Rev. Powers was in critical condition. He was moved to a hospital in Asheville, North Carolina, to receive more specialized care.

The congregation of Meadow Creek rose to the tragic challenge. George stayed at the Miller's. Congregation members cared for Margie, brought food and clothing, and helped her go back to school. They continued to support the family financially during the long and difficult recovery process. They worked for days cleaning up the family home from fire and smoke damage.

Paul Allen Powers was buried next to his mother. And the family was again challenged to remember and live out their father's words, "Tomorrow still comes whether you want it to or not. You can wallow in self-pity or you can look around and see three people in worse shape than yourself."

It took many tomorrows for Janice to heal. It took even more tomorrows for Rev. Powers to recover. He was hospitalized from November till January, 1964, and after he recovered from his burns, he suffered kidney disease and lost a kidney in April. When the doctors recommended that he retire and take it easy, he scoffed at the notion. He knew that there were "three people worse off" than he who needed his help.

In 1965, Rev. Powers left Meadow Creek and moved on to implement his three-point program at another small church in Yancey County, North Carolina. He moved to Micaville with Janice and George. He continued to minister to Presbyterian churches in Yancey County until he finally retired in 1997.

Johnny remained in Greene County and at Meadow Creek. He was in love with Lois Birdwell, and Rev. Powers returned and performed their wedding ceremony. Johnny and Lois remain stalwart members of Meadow Creek. Johnny has served as deacon and elder for most of his adult life. He served on the committee that built the Fellowship Hall and the Anniversary Committee in 1987. Lois has been very active in teaching Sunday School and serving as an officer of the Women's Bible Study. Johnny and Lois's son, John Stephen, serves as head deacon and Sunday School Superintendent. Their grandson, John Stephen Powers, is an active teenage member of Meadow Creek, as is his brother Mitchell. Rev. John Powers came to Meadow Creek in 1960 and his legacy lives on. For the next fifty years, there have been two or three men named John Powers in Meadow Creek. They all share a dedication to build up the church and serve the community. Their lives represent another example of God's providence and faithfulness to His covenant.

Johnny Powers will always hate fire and has fought it all his life, serving now as the Chief of the South Greene Volunteer Fire Department. (He still has the FFA jacket with the burn marks acquired when he used it to try to smother the flames on his father.)

Janice re-joined Meadow Creek with her husband, Jerry Hoyle, in 2000. Janice and Jerry always volunteer for fellowship activities. Janice has worked on special audio-video productions for Veteran's Day services, and currently serves on the Cemetery Committee and the History Committee. Because of her motivational abilities, she is affectionately known as "Number Two," a nickname given to her by her nephew to acknowledge her behind-the-scenes leadership. (She's #2 behind the pastor.) The Hoyle's daughter, Elaine Stewart and her family are very active in Sunday School and Youth Group activities. Elaine's husband Brian has worked on the current church renovation, especially laying all the new tiles in the basement, and in repairing tomb rocks in the cemetery. Haile, Kaelynn, and Hannah have shared their musical and dramatic talents at most of the church's special programs. The whole Stewart family devotes many hours and much energy to Youth Group activities.

So, fifty years after his arrival, five of Rev. Powers' great-grandchildren remain actively involved at Meadow Creek.

After serving the Lord and His people all of his life, Rev. Powers died in 2005 at the age of ninety-two. He's buried next to Esther and Paul. Four days before he died, his last words to Margie were, "We've had a lot of joy in life, haven't we Margie?"

Margie, Johnny, Janice, and George all spoke of the difficulties of being "Preacher's Kids." They were always in the spotlight, and some people had no trouble complaining to the pastor about their behavior. Their dad expected a lot from them and often warned them, "If you embarrass me, I'll embarrass you." They didn't like the burden of having to set a good example.

> *Margie said of her dad that "he had the best personality. He always thought the best of people and brought out the best in them."*
>
> *George remembers his great sense of humor. He tells the story of one hog-killing time when they were still at Cedar Creek. When the butchering was finished, Rev. Powers wrapped the pig's ear in gift wrap and gave it to Hazel Humphries for Christmas. He did not put his name on the gift. But when Hazel opened it, others questioned her as to who would give her such a thing. Hazel replied, "That darned old preacher gave it to me."*
>
> *She saved it, re-wrapped it, and returned it to Rev. Powers the following Christmas.*

Johnny also remembers how frequently his mother prayed "that the Lord would use her and us kids to be a strength for Daddy in his ministry and be good examples for others." All of the Powers children knew that the Lord was watching over them and watching out for them. But they had a hard time understanding why such bad things happened to them at such a young age.

They also spoke of the difficulty of following their dad's example. Over the years, each of them questioned their father about why God took their mother when they needed her so much. Why did Paul have to die?

How could Dad remain steadfast, faithful, and optimistic? Janice finally understood the source of her father's strength when he spoke his last words to her, "Always remember Jani, all of you are loved each and every day." Tomorrows always come, bringing with them still more steadfast love.

Johnny and George remarked about the depth of their father's close personal relationship with the Lord. Rev. Powers reminded his children that they had a source of comfort and strength. By example, he showed his family, his congregation, and his community that God doesn't stop tragic events from hurting His people, but He does provide the strength, courage, and joy to face each tomorrow.

The Powers Family in January, 2010:

George and Johnny Powers
Janice Powers Hoyle and Margie Powers Tilley

Descendants of Rev. and Mrs. Powers still at Meadow Creek:

Front: Haile Stewart, Mitchell Powers, Rachel Crum, Julia Crum
Middle: Brian Stewart, Elaine Stewart, Kaelynn Stewart, Heath
Crum Mike Crum.
Back: Jerry Hoyle, Janice Hoyle, Brye Powers, John Stephan
Powers, John Stephan Powers, Lois Powers, John Powers.

"A Little Fish in a Big Pond"

Meadow Creek Presbyterian Church is a small country church that belongs to a large Presbyterian denomination. As such, it has had little influence on the various controversies that occurred within the denomination. Instead, it had to adapt to events largely beyond its control. It sometimes had to make choices about which side of a controversy to support. Those choices would have an impact upon its church life.

In 1801, Presbyterians united with Congregationalists, uniting the two largest Calvinistic denominations within the United States. That union was not without controversy and created theological tensions that lasted until 1837. Two factions developed because of those tensions, and they were known as the Old School and the New School. Besides theological issues, the approach to missions was another point of contention and it was the most important one for Meadow Creek. The Old School faction favored denominational control of missions whereas the New School faction favored supporting the American Home Missionary Society as well as Presbyterian home missions.

In 1837, the first year that Meadow Creek was an organized church, the Old School Faction expelled the New School Faction from the Presbyterian Church in the United States. So, Meadow Creek had to choose which faction to be aligned with. Since the New School faction favored a broader and more open approach to missions, and Meadow Creek had benefited from denominational support of mission churches, Meadow Creek went New School. This allegiance meant that the church moved from the French Broad Presbytery (Old School) to the Holston Presbytery (New School). That relationship lasted from 1839-1857. (Meadow Creek History, 1987)

When the issue of slavery split Presbyterianism yet again into anti- and pro-slavery factions, Meadow Creek chose to stay in the Holston Presbytery, which moved to the United Synod of the Presbyterian Church in the USA, a group that sought to avoid discussing the issue of slavery because it was so divisive and highly charged. The United

Synod was an attempt to remain neutral about the slavery because it was dividing the denomination into Northern and Southern groups. The United Synod's position was that slavery was not necessarily sinful but also was not desirable. This position was reflective of the realities of East Tennessee where slavery existed, but was not widespread. It was also reflective of the realities at Meadow Creek, which had three slaves and their families in its membership, but the majority of members did not own slaves. (Meadow Creek History, and Session Books)

After the Civil War the Presbyterian Church faced many organizational difficulties. Many different groups organized along political beliefs rather than Scriptural or theological beliefs. When it all got sorted out after the war, Meadow Creek voted to "declare ourselves in connection with the Presbytery of Holston of the Synod of Nashville of the Presbyterian Church in the United States." (April 17, 1869 entry in Session Book) Meadow Creek was a congregation in that denomination from 1869-1973.

The relationship between the little church and the larger denomination was focused mainly on the need for good preaching. The small size of the congregation meant that it could not support a full-time pastor and had to depend upon the denomination supplying preachers who could preach at various churches within a geographical region for a certain period of time. They were essentially circuit-riders who depended upon the contributions of two to five churches for their support. Besides the financial benefit to Meadow Creek, the congregation could also be assured that their preachers were well-trained and properly examined for Scriptural and doctrinal knowledge.

The denominational relationship also meant that Meadow Creek could combine its limited resources with other churches to support missions and educational programs. The denomination provided literature for study groups, also. Another benefit of belonging to the large denomination was that the membership of individuals and families was transferable. Finally, quarterly Presbytery meetings provided an opportunity for the elders of small churches to help each other with problems and hold each other accountable for maintaining high standards of preaching, teaching, and church life.

However, the Presbyterian Church in the United States was not immune to cultural forces in America at large. In the post World War II era, Protestant churches faced many stresses and strains. As American society became more and more secular, the church faced criticism and even ridicule for its definitions of sexual morality, its adherence to the infallibility and inerrancy of Scripture, its belief in creation as opposed to evolution, and its practices of Sabbath observance, and its understanding about the role of women in church leadership. A majority of Presbyterians wanted to be more accommodating to the culture. A more conservative minority was determined to follow the Bible rather than the society at large. So, in 1973, a new Presbyterian denomination was formed and took the name, Presbyterian Church in America.

Because Meadow Creek had always tried to be faithful in attending to denominational matters, the congregation was very aware of the changes occurring within the denomination. They were very concerned about what to do. Meadow Creek sent representatives to Presbytery meetings regularly almost every quarter. In February of 1969, the Session considered joining the Reformed Presbyterian Church, and in November it discussed a letter from Concerned Presbyterians of Atlanta about "changes being considered by a biblical movement." Meadow Creek's representatives to Presbytery were instructed to vote against the move to enlarge and reorganize Presbyteries. They were "very opposed to the denomination's membership in the World Council of Churches." By October of 1970, the session sent three officers of the church to a meeting in Johnson City for Concerned Presbyterians.

By April of 1973, things started to come to a head. Meadow Creek's pulpit would be vacant by May 31 as Thomas McClelland had resigned to attend seminary. The denomination recommended one older man, but Meadow Creek was interested in the much younger Larry Ball, who strongly supported the more conservative Concerned Presbyterians. Since Meadow Creek and New Ebenezer, its "daughter" church, shared pastoral expenses, there were many joint meetings to discuss who to call and what to do about denominational concerns. Darwyn Waddell was delegated to attend the Advisory Convention of the Concerned Presbyterians held August 7-9, 1973.

At the Session meeting of August 12, elders Darwyn Waddell, Haynes Gammon, Paul Hensley, Boyce Gammon, and Ivan Ward, Jr. decided to call a congregational meeting for August 26 to vote on Meadow Creek's withdrawal from the Holston Presbytery after almost 125 years of membership. Four years of discussions and meetings had gone into this decision because it meant so much. They prepared a resolution listing twelve reasons for their decision to terminate this membership, seven of which dealt with biblical and doctrinal issues, two with organizational issues, and three with social issues.

There are thirty Presbyterian churches in Greene County, fifteen of which are from the Cumberland Presbyterian denomination, a denomination predominately found in Kentucky and Tennessee. By choosing to leave the PCUSA, Meadow Creek would be leaving the close denominational relationship with Timber Ridge, Mt. Zion, Cedar Creek, and New Ebenezer churches. New Ebenezer also wanted to leave, but the Holston Presbytery held title to their property. If they left the denomination, they would also lose their church building, so they couldn't go with Meadow Creek.

Meadow Creek's decision was not lightly taken and much time and prayer went into it. They waited until it was a unanimous decision for both the Session and the congregation.

All the elders signed the following statement:

> *We, the duly elected elders and officers of this church, having taken solemn vows to be zealous in maintaining the purity of the church and particularly the work of God entrusted unto us here at Meadow Creek Church, herewith go on record before Almighty God and all His angels, and all men and reaffirm our faith in the Bible as the Word of God, the only infallible rule of faith and practice; and further reaffirm that our main and primary allegiance is to Jesus Christ, the great head of the church, rather than to any denominational group itself; and accordingly we pledge to stand united in the mighty name of God, standing on His Word alone, trusting in His mighty arms, and furthermore we covenant and promise to stand true to the congregation of this Church to stand without*

> *wavering . . . willing, ready and determined to come out and*
> *stand for our God and His truth. August 26, 1973*

The resolution listing the twelve reasons for their decision to terminate their membership in the Presbyterian Church in the United States was presented to the congregation. At the meeting the vote was 39-0 in support of the resolution. To underscore the seriousness of the issue, each member signed the vote which stated:

> *We the Undersigned active members of Meadow Creek*
> *Presbyterian Church, hereby band together, our trust being*
> *in our Lord God and in the written Word, the Bible, in its*
> *fullness and entirety, do confess and stand together as a united*
> *family of believers, and herewith go on record that we . . . on*
> *our free choice and conviction . . . are in favor of and vote for*
> *coming out from the denomination "The Presbyterian Church*
> *in the United States." August 26, 1973*

Needless to say, Holston Presbytery was greatly grieved by these developments and attempted to deal with the issues raised. But it was too late. Too much prayer and discussion had gone into the decision and there was no turning back although Holston would not remove Meadow Creek from its rolls for two more years.

Since 1973, the PCUSA has declined in membership. Meadow Creek has become a member of the Westminster Presbytery of the Presbyterian Church in America, and since 1973, the PCA has experienced growth in membership.

Meadow Creek is still a little country church within a large denomination, but it has tried to remain true to its doctrinal roots and faithful to the Scriptures. Throughout its 200 year history, Meadow Creek has been affiliated with five different Presbyterian denominations. It is the 31st oldest Presbyterian Church in the United States, but its membership has never been much more than one hundred. They have tried to adhere to the scriptures and live out the Westminster Confession's statement, "to know God and enjoy Him forever." God has been faithful to them. It was and is a covenantal relationship.

The Challenging Role of Preacher

For the first one hundred years, the preachers at Meadow Creek were supplied by Presbytery. These intrepid circuit riders preached to Meadow Creek, Timber Ridge, Mount Zion and/or Cedar Creek, small country churches scattered throughout Greene County. Many of these early preachers were trained at Princeton, which served as the Presbyterian Seminary before it became an Ivy-League university. Some preachers graduated from the local Presbyterian college, Tusculum, which aspired to be the "Princeton of the Frontier." Most preachers couldn't stay in the area for too long, especially if they had families, as the pay was insufficient and living conditions were harsh.

The years 1861-1865 saw a total breakdown of civilian society in the region. During the Civil War, the churches in East Tennessee stopped holding services altogether. Not only were political loyalties divided, but it simply wasn't safe to leave home to go to church, or ride the circuit as a single preacher. Travel was hazardous and leaving the homeplace undefended was foolish. Union and Confederate raiders would commandeer or steal livestock and food stuffs. Deserters and bushwackers would harass and threaten travelers. It was a time to hunker down and worship at the family altar. Meadow Creek's preacher, John Blackburn, was driven from the area by Union backers because he supported the Confederates.

During the post-war era, Greene County suffered such economic depression that churches had to band together to collect enough resources to support a preacher. Meadow Creek often shared the expenses of a preacher with Mount Zion and Cedar Creek Presbyterian Churches. However, by about 1900, the relationship between preacher and congregation changed. The elders of Meadow Creek thought that the church was large enough and financially able to support a pastor and his family. The congregation committed to building a manse, so that they could offer their preacher a home. Because the preacher was now available to the congregation all week, and not just on Sundays, he would be a pastor to them, especially during times of sickness and death. (The distinction between "preacher" and "pastor" comes from their job descriptions. Preachers deliver a sermon or instruct the congregation.

Pastors are considered to be like shepherds, leading and guiding the members as they face the challenges of life.)

The manse was completed in 1909 and the Rev. James Alexander Thompson was the first preacher to live next to the church. He was now accessible to everyone who needed him. However, living in the country meant that access to good medical care was difficult and his wife was sickly, so for the sake of his wife's health, Rev. Thompson had to leave. The same was true of his successor, Rev. John Wood. When his wife, Leonora, became pregnant with their daughter, Catherine, they too moved on. (Catherine grew up to be Catherine Marshall who wrote the best-seller *Christy*, a novel based upon the lives of her parents, Rev. John and Leonora Wood.)

In the post-Civil War era many business transactions involved bartering, and preaching at Meadow Creek was no exception. The congregation reasoned that they couldn't pay a competitive salary, but they could provide a manse, fields in which to grow vegetables, and wood for the furnace. But even those tangible benefits were often not enough to compensate for a lack of cash. In 1920, after three years of service, Rev. Pearman notified the Session that he had to leave and stated his reason as "inadequate support." Meadow Creek then had to rely on the services of home missionary, John Martin for two years. Home Missionaries were subsidized by the denomination. When he left in 1922, Meadow Creek's pulpit was vacant for three more years. Finally the Session talked Rev. Pearman into returning in 1925. He only stayed for two more years of service.

Since 1945 most of the preachers who came to Meadow Creek were fresh out of the seminary. They only stayed from three to five years and gained important pastoral experience. They generally moved on to bigger churches.

For example, Rev. James Richter had just graduated from the seminary in 1982. Previously he had spent many years of his working life in the engineering field and went back to the seminary because he felt called by God to be a pastor. Rev. Richter also liked living in the country, growing vegetables, and going hunting. He described the seven years he spent at

Meadow Creek as "very beneficial" because pastoring a small country church taught him the practical "life" lessons that can't be learned in the seminary. He could get to know each member of the small congregation more intimately and had fewer of the administrative demands of a larger church. He also found that he had more time to study and gain knowledge as well as experience.

During his seven years at Meadow Creek, 1982-1989, the Fellowship Hall was built and the 175th Anniversary was celebrated. He credits Boyce Gammon with leading the very successful fund drive and remembers that each member contributed their labor to the project.

Rev. Richter learned that small churches are "very vulnerable to the impact of disagreements and strife." Each member of the congregation is so very important to the communal worship and overall spiritual health of the congregation. Therefore, he recognized how vitally important it is to not only be faithful to the scriptures, but also to work for peace and harmony in the church family. When Rev. Richter left in 1989 to go to a larger church in Alabama, the congregation was sad to see him go.

In fact, throughout its 200 year history, most preachers left under amicable circumstances as they moved on to larger congregations with greater resources. With the dawn of the 21st Century, however, two preachers left Meadow Creek under unhappy circumstances. Disagreements over church government and forms of worship became personal conflicts between each preacher and the congregation. Unable to achieve peace, these men sought to assert their authority. That made things worse and those conflicts proved Rev. Richter's concern about the vulnerability of small congregations. Attendance on Sunday fell, and the collection plate held smaller and smaller amounts. Fears about the viability of the church grew within the remaining members. Finally, Westminster Presbytery's Shepherding Committee had to get involved to affect the separations from Rev. Thornton and Rev. Van Blerk. These conflicts were very demoralizing to the members of Meadow Creek and hurtful to each preacher. It was very sad. In the years 2000-2007, members left the congregation, and the church was smaller in 2007 than it had been when it was first organized in 1837.

Elizabeth, Robin, Victoria, Joel and Benjamin

However, even in these times of turmoil, God was watching out for his people. At this very low point in its history, seminarian Joel Kennedy came to Meadow Creek for two summers in 2000 and 2001. During the vacancy in 2007-2008, he was again able to help. He and his family commuted from Maryville every Sunday. Joel was a kind and loving man, and along with his warm-hearted wife, Robin, was able to help heal hurt feelings and keep the tiny congregation together. The congregation remains very grateful for his pastoral care.

The challenges faced by the congregation at Meadow Creek are just as daunting as those faced by the generation that started the church in 1812, or the generation that rebuilt after the Civil War. That first generation had to create a community in the wilderness. They had to struggle to survive, and their faith strengthened them. The second generation had few resources but great resilience, and their faith helped heal them. The current generation wants to reach out to a community that lives in the wilderness of commercialism and secularism. The trend in current American Christianity is to belong to the big mega-churches with many social programs. Even in rural Greene County, the large churches in town attract the young families much more than a little red-brick country church located on a hilltop off the beaten path.

But Meadow Creek can offer benefits other than large social programs and activities. As its current history has proven, each member is very important to the spiritual health and well-being of the whole congregation. Each member's opinion and contribution is appreciated. And each member can be assured of having not only a preacher, but also a pastor who has the time to get to know them well.

For its first one hundred years, Meadow Creek had a series of preachers, men whose sole responsibility was to preach the gospel, perform baptisms, weddings and funerals, and administer the sacraments. For its second hundred years, the relationship between preacher and congregation expanded into a pastoral relationship whereby the congregation committed to providing for the pastor's physical needs while he was expected to be teacher, counselor, and mentor as well as preacher.

For its first one hundred years, Meadow Creek paid preachers sent by Presbytery. The system of calling a pastor to the church by the congregation is a modern development, which has its own drawbacks, as there are many inherent conflicts in the Presbyterian form of church government. The pastor is dependent upon the congregation for financial support but must provide leadership in spiritual matters. The pastor must be both employee and father-figure. He must respond to the emotional and spiritual needs of the congregation, but members can choose to ignore his teachings. He is expected to provide leadership, but members can choose not to follow. Therefore, pastors need the patience of Job, the wisdom of Solomon, and the preaching skills of Paul to do the work.

Throughout the years, there have always been men willing to take on the challenge. The Lord has always provided for Meadow Creek.

Jeffrey, Carey and Rev. Jeff Neikirk

And in 2007, the pastoral search committee received a letter from a fifty year old man who had just graduated from the seminary. He was raised in the city, but held a Bachelors degree in agriculture. He had been a deacon, elder and youth pastor. He left the world of business because he felt called to be a pastor.

When he came to visit, the congregation thought he was an excellent Sunday School teacher and a good preacher. They voted to call him to be the thirty-ninth preacher and pastor. Pastor Jeff Neikirk answered Meadow Creek's call. His many life experiences preceding his ministry have enabled him to be a good pastor as well as a good preacher. He sees his duty as preaching an "historical faith to a new generation."

For its third one hundred years Meadow Creek Presbyterian Church has adopted for its motto:

"Not to us, O Lord, not to us,
But to thy name give glory, for the sake of thy steadfast love
and thy faithfulness."
Psalm 155:1

Bequests to Meadow Creek Presbyterian Church

In the history of Meadow Creek, there is perhaps no greater example of God's Providence than in the way He has provided for the financial needs of the church. For 200 years, the church has remained debt-free because of a series of bequests and the volunteer labor of the members.

In 1812, Michael Woods was an elder of the Timber Ridge Presbyterian Church. It was a long, hard ride by horseback to get there after first fording the unpredictable and often dangerous Nolichucky River. He and his neighbors, the Cochrans, Greggs, Marshalls, Crawfords, and others had many children who needed to be raised in the "fear of the Lord." They needed to be taught to read and write, even though they lived in the wilderness. They needed to learn how to be good citizens. So, he set aside some of his land, called upon his neighbors for help, and built a two-story log structure. It was named, Meadow Creek Academy. The children attended classes during the week, and whole families came together on Sundays to worship God under the preaching of circuit-riding preachers. Michael Woods was an elder of one church, but God used him to start another church that would meet the needs of the community. Because God used Michael Woods to provide the land and the first structure, Meadow Creek Presbyterian Church began its ministry free of any debt. That freedom from debt has remained a characteristic of the church to modern times.

In 1844, the Meadow Creek Congregation relocated the meeting house to the intersection of Gregg Mill Road and Allens Bridge Road on land given by the Cochran family. The site was on a small hilltop with a panoramic view of the mountains. Church members worked together and instead of a two-story log house, the church building from 1844-1852 was a simple frame building filled with sun-dried bricks and weather-boarded from the outside. There are no records of payment to anyone for the construction of this meeting house, so it is reasonable to assume that the self-sufficient and handy farmers of the congregation contributed their skills and labor to build the frame and make the bricks.

Beginning in 1852, the congregation desired to construct a bigger and better church. It would take a long time to make the bricks and shingles.

The four years of Civil War and the post-war years of a ruined economy would stop all progress. Sometime during the 1870s a man named Mr. Shackleford exchanged his labor for shelter. He lived in the old church while he built a new brick church. The interior walls were plastered. The floor was made from wooden planks, as were the pews. (Meadow Creek History, 1987)

God used the gifts of His people to build His church. Hand-made bricks and hand-hewn timbers were used to build a simple church on donated land under the shade of an oak tree.

Meadow Creek began to grow, both from natural increase and because of special revival meetings. During the late 1890s, the church reached its peak of membership: about 100. Around 1890, a red belfry was added to the church and its large bell pealed out the call to worship and announced the deaths of members.

And in 1893, Miss Catherine Hale, a sister of Eliza Hale Cochran, wrote her last will and testament. Catherine Hale managed a seventy-two acre farm. Her will stipulated that it be left to her siblings until their deaths when it would become the property of Meadow Creek Church. She wrote, "I hereby direct that my farm shall be repaired and improved all it can be, so that its value may increase and the church of the living God may have all that my prosperity may bring to it." Catherine Hale died in 1904.

Her bequest reflected her belief that Meadow Creek should continue to grow and prosper. In 1908, James Allen (son of "Devil Jim"), W. K. Mitchell, and N. T. Chambers received a quick claim deed to the land. But, for the next sixteen years, that land would be a source of much controversy. Managing the land would become a burden to members who had to work very hard just to manage their own farms.

The choice was between selling the land immediately or renting it out. The congregation was divided, but the majority favored renting it out. Of course that made them landlords. And, they had a difficult time finding responsible renters and keeping the farm in good repair. During the course of those sixteen years, tensions between church members grew in intensity. For example, in 1916, the supply pastor for Meadow Creek, Rev. H. H. Cassidy focused much of the blame for the arguments about their rental property on Mr. N. T. Chambers, an elder. Because of this public criticism, Mr. Chambers and his family left Meadow Creek.

Then Rev. Cassidy left Meadow Creek in early 1917. On May 14, 1917, the Session called a special meeting moderated by Frank Hunt from Holston Presbytery:

> " . . . *the purpose of this meeting for conference concerning differences and troubles that have arisen in the church, and among the officers, to such an extent as to produce lack of harmony and serious discord and faction, injurious to the church life and work.*
>
> "*He (Frank D. Hunt, Moderator) suggested that instead of going into any discussions of the details of the situation and trouble, which are all so fully known to each one present, the best and most effective way to restore harmony and peace would be for each officer present to express himself here and now as willing to forgive anyone who may have said or done*

anything that wronged him, or hurt his feelings, and also to ask forgiveness of everyone whose feelings he had hurt in any way, or wronged in any way.

This suggestion was unanimously accepted and each elder and deacon present (James Allen, D. L. Woods, J. A. Waddell, N. T. Chambers, J. A. Cochran, V. R. Hawk, and Robert Rupert) arose and spoke accordingly. Whereupon the Moderator declared that by this action, the past discord was forgiven and blotted out and that peace and harmony were restored.

All then knelt in prayer, and several led in prayer thanking God for His grace and guidance in bringing these results to pass."

These words paint a powerful picture of strong-willed men of the land humbling themselves to each other, forgiving and asking forgiveness of each other, and kneeling in prayer before their God. But it's important to remember that these men were also strong-willed Presbyterians. They have a very high regard for doing things according to the rules of the church, also known as the Book of Church Order. On May 18, 1917, another Session Meeting was called because it turned out that Rev. Cassidy had never been a member of any Presbytery of the Southern Presbyterian Church. So, the question was raised, "Since he wasn't a member of any Presbytery, were any of his actions legal?" Holston Presbytery responded in September that meetings held under the moderation of Rev. Cassidy were indeed legal.

Finally, on May 30, 1920, the Session presented a special resolution to the congregation:

"Resolved: That during the time the church was supplied by Rev. Cassidy that N. T. Chambers was attacked in an uncalled for manner by the said Cassidy in public in the church and among other charges, alleged that the said Chambers had been a disturbance in the church for twelve years. Now we, the Session of Meadow Creek Church, condemn this attack

on Bro. Chambers as malicious and uncalled for and cordially invite Bro. Chambers and wife to return to church and resume their church work."

The congregation approved the resolution. During Mr. Chambers' absence, the congregation had also voted, on August 5th, 1919, to dispose of the Hale Farm "by public auction as speedily as possible."

The problems with the Hale Farm were not over yet. The property would not be sold until 1926. For sixteen years, a blessed bequest had been a source of conflict and unending responsibility. How could this story be an example of God's Providence? How could this blessing of land and rental income turn into something detrimental to the peace and harmony of the congregation?

During the sixteen years spent managing the Hale Farm, the bell in the red belfry cracked. It was taken down and never replaced. The church built by Mr. Shackleford aged and deteriorated during the same time that disharmony grew within the congregation. The mortar began to crack. The walls of the church were being pushed apart by the weight of the roof. They attempted to stabilize the walls by inserting large metal rods, spanning through the sanctuary, but it didn't work. Finally, in response to concerns for safety, the old brick church was abandoned. The congregation again met in a school house, the Mt. Zion School, a short distance up Allens Bridge Road.

In 1926, a committee was formed to tear down the old church. In July of 1928, C. J. Waddell bought the Hale land for $2500. Mr. N. T. Chambers pledged $5,000 toward a new church. Misters James Allen, Charles Waddell, James A. Waddell, W. K. Mitchell, W. B. Hawk, and Ivan Ward, Sr. served as the building committee.

The first services in the new brick sanctuary took place on April 1, 1929. This new sanctuary was now located at the rear of the cemetery rather than at the front. And, this new brick church was shaded by a very large, sturdy oak tree in the churchyard.

All the strong-willed Presbyterian men involved in this story struggled with seeing where God was leading them. Receiving the Hale bequest in 1908 and maintaining the property for sixteen years in spite of arguments and conflict, meant that the funds necessary for the construction of a new sanctuary were available in 1928. The largest donor to that fund was the man at the center of the controversy, Mr. N. T. Chambers. The men involved may have spoken harsh words, but they had also spoken words of forgiveness and been driven to their knees in communal prayer. Reading the historical record clearly reveals God's Providence to Meadow Creek Church. And a knowledge of history shows that when the Great Depression began a mere six months after the first worship service in the new sanctuary, Meadow Creek Church was still debt free.

The Chambers Bequest: In 1938, Florence Chambers, the wife of N. T. Chambers, purchased a $2,000 annuity, the proceeds of which were to go for the upkeep of the cemetery. For seventy-two years, Meadow

Creek Church has received an annual check averaging about $250 for the maintenance of the cemetery in which she and N. T. Chambers are buried. Florence Chambers was also a descendant of Marshall Gregg, a charter member of Meadow Creek.

The Susong Bequest: In 1946, Ethel Gregg Susong created a trust fund with $1,000. The income from that trust was used for the next sixty years to maintain the graves of the Greggs and the Chambers and to add to the pastor's salary.

While the men of Meadow Creek donated labor and materials, it is interesting that all the financial bequests to Meadow Creek Church were made by women. Besides the bequests of Catherine Hale, Florence Chambers and Ethel Susong, Fannie Kiser, Launa Crum, and Winnie Wilhoit named Meadow Creek Church as beneficiaries in their wills. And the largest bequest of all came from a woman who never attended Meadow Creek, Mrs. Hester King.

The King Bequest, 2010

In the spring of 1985 Ralph and Hester King walked into Russell's Hardware store in downtown Greeneville. They wanted a push mower and a riding mower in matching colors. The sales clerk, Janice Hoyle, worked hard to meet their needs and desires. The King's were impressed with her knowledge of the equipment and her excellent customer service. In fact years later Hester King would say of her, "That young girl could have run that whole place."

The King's had just moved to Greeneville from California. Ralph King was born in Greeneville, but left as a young man. Hester originated from Ohio, met Ralph on the train to California, and married him there. When they retired, they came back to Ralph's hometown.

Over the years, the Kings always traded at whatever store Janice Hoyle could be found. They trusted her and appreciated the way she treated her customers. As the years went on, their health deteriorated. They never had any children together, so, they were alone, getting feeble, and in need of a caring friend.

When Hester broke her hip, Ralph realized that they would have to make major changes in their lifestyle. He decided they should sell their home and move into Wellington Place, an assisted living facility. As a result of that decision, Ralph called Janice to tell her they wouldn't need her to service their lawn mowers anymore. She was only trying to be polite when she asked, "Do you need some help?" Ralph may have hoped she would say that, because he asked her to help them pack and move.

She did not plan to spend her day off doing that, but she kept her word. That was the beginning of requests for help that the Kings made of Janice. On a weekly basis, she was running errands for them whether it was to the post office, banks, or stores. Once they were settled in, Janice would come and visit. Soon they were calling her frequently.

Ralph King died first. Then one day, in 2007, when Janice came to visit her, Hester asked Janice to make a list of small country churches who could use some financial help. Hester was in her nineties and she wanted to put her affairs in order. Hester wanted her estate to go to help other people. She had a particular interest in small churches, having grown up in one.

Hester went over Janice's list with Attorney Jeff Cobble who was writing her new will. Janice had included Meadow Creek on the list and the attorney advised Hester that Meadow Creek was Janice's church.

Hester King died in 2009. When Attorney Cobble read Hester's will to Janice, she learned, for the first time, that Meadow Creek Presbyterian Church would receive a portion of that total. The other beneficiaries of Hester King were Princeton Community Church of Ohio, a church she remembered from her childhood, Freedom Baptist Church in Greeneville, the YMCA, and the Greeneville-Greene County Community Ministries Food Bank. Because the Princeton Community Church no longer existed, its share was divided up and passed to the other two churches. Meadow Creek Presbyterian Church would receive over a quarter of a million dollars.

In many ways, the King bequest illustrates God's Providence very clearly. Through a series of events, over the lifetimes of Hester King and Janice Hoyle, God blessed Meadow Creek Presbyterian Church.

Janice Powers Hoyle was just a young woman working hard at her job when the Kings walked into the store. Because she "always tried to be good to my customers," a business relationship based on trust developed between Janice Hoyle and the Kings. Late in her life, Hester depended upon that relationship.

Why did Janice take her lunch hours to run errands for the Kings? Why did she accept the responsibility of caring for her old neighbors and customers?

Janice was raised as a "preacher's kid." Rev. Powers taught her and her siblings to help people that needed help by making them work with tobacco farmers. So with that training, she really didn't think much about helping the Kings. She just did what needed to be done. She certainly had not planned to become as involved as she did with Ralph and Hester King, but as she said, "I just sort of liked them because they were different. They were eccentric people."

On many occasions, Janice Hoyle would have rather gone anywhere but Wellington Place. Sometimes "loving your neighbor" can be tedious. But Attorney Cobble reminded her, "You're the only person she's got here, and she trusts you."

Why did Hester King ask Janice Hoyle to provide a list of small, country churches to be her beneficiaries? Hester was one of six children and her father could not adequately provide for the family. So Hester was taken in by an aunt and uncle when she was fourteen. They insisted that she go to church, the Princeton Community Church. They stressed the values of honesty and generosity, and they sent her to business college so she could be self-sufficient.

While Hester was not a church-goer in her adulthood, she always cared about people struggling to get along. She was very generous to others all her life, especially "deserving" people. And Hester King found Janice Hoyle to be very deserving because, as Carol Cobble of the Freedom Baptist Church described their relationship, "She loved Janice like a daughter." Carol Cobble didn't hesitate to affirm, "If Janice had not done what she did for the Kings, I don't know what would have happened to them."

The Bible clearly teaches that God has a plan for his people. God provides and protects. He gave Janice a servant's heart and the physical strength to help the Kings in their final years. He then used the lifetime accumulations of the Kings to feed the hungry, provide for the young, and bless the ministry of two country churches in Greene County.

The King Bequest arrived at Meadow Creek Presbyterian Church at a time when the walls of the eighty year old brick church had cracked and pulled away from the foundation because of two years of severe drought. Stabilizing the foundation would require $16,000. Strong storms during the winter of 2009-2010 damaged the roof. New roofs are very costly. The walls needed repair and repainting. The carpeting was over thirty years old. Those expensive repairs and renovations could now be made without mortgaging the property. The eighty year old interior could be restored to excellent condition and Meadow Creek could remain debt free. A committee of volunteers would work through all the details.

Beginning in the spring of 2010, when the King bequest was received, the basement walls were stabilized, the roof was repaired, the sanctuary was rewired, re-plastered, and repainted. The basement has new tile flooring and the sanctuary has new carpeting. The pews have new cushions. All of these renovations could be accomplished without borrowing a cent.

Besides upgrading the fourth sanctuary of a church approaching its bicentennial, the King Bequest serves as a challenge to the people of Meadow Creek to develop new ways to be good neighbors to the South Greene community. A great bequest is also a great challenge. How will God work continue to work for the good of those who love Him?

God's Providence

People experience life day-by-day. When confronted by problems or tragic events, it is often difficult to deal with them because there is no easy answer to the question, "WHY?" If Christians truly believe that God is in control of all of life, then they also have to believe that He has a plan and a purpose for everything that happens. The Bible teaches us that God's plan is the redemption of His people in order to bring them into a closer fellowship with Him. Everything that happens in life conforms to that long-range plan. Therefore, only a long-range view of human events can lead to an understanding of God's providence.

That is why a study of the history of a people or an institution can be helpful to strengthening faith. There is no doubt that the stories of Meadow Creek are the stories of sinners. They did wrong. They made mistakes. They hurt each other. But the story of redemption also shines through their lives.

These are not the stories of great leaders or heroic characters. Even the problems they faced have been faced by people everywhere. Disagreement and discord can be found in all human relationships. Everyone will face death. The writer of Ecclesiastes summed it up very simply, " . . . there is nothing new under the sun . . . . I know that whatever God does endures for ever; nothing can be added to it, nor anything taken from it; God has made it so, in order that men should fear before him." (Ecclesiastes. 1:9, 3:14)

People of faith started a church in the wilderness. People of faith struggled day by day through four years of destructive Civil War and social anarchy. When confronted by a murder within the congregation, committed by one of its leaders, people of faith kept their counsel and nurtured the victims. When confronted by the tragedies of cancer and a deadly fire that tormented a beloved pastor and his family, the congregation worked through it all one day at a time by focusing on meeting the family's physical and spiritual needs. When confronted by the need to choose which form of Presbyterianism to belong to, Meadow Creek studied the issues, spent much time in prayer, and chose to follow the teachings of Scripture.

None of the Christians involved in dealing with these problems knew how their decisions would affect the solution to their problems. They simply did their best and trusted God to do the rest.

Meadow Creek exists, but not just because of Michael Woods, Samuel Cochran, or Marshall Gregg. Meadow Creek recovered from the Civil War and doubled in size during the next generation, but not because of any one preacher or teacher. "Devil Jim" Allen was ruined financially but redeemed spiritually. Nellie Houston lived a long and productive life as a faithful Christian and devoted wife and mother, not because she was so good, but because she was so blessed. Descendants of Rev. Powers still follow his example of strength and courage, not because he was a perfect father, but because they know that strength and courage comes from God. Broken relationships with two different preachers allowed God to work through Dr. Kennedy and eventually Rev. Neikirk to keep Meadow Creek moving forward.

In an age when many churches take on mortgages and struggle to meet rich budgets, Meadow Creek has always been, and continues to be, not only free of debt, but richly endowed with financial freedom. Good stewardship has not always been easy, but it has always been necessary and blessed.

No one man, no one family, no human plan has achieved these things. The only constant throughout 200 years has been the faithfulness of God.

Chapter Three
Branches of God's Family Tree

The magnificent red oak in the churchyard of Meadow Creek Presbyterian Church not only has deep roots and a strong sturdy trunk, it also has branches that extend out in all directions. The tree in the churchyard truly is a metaphor for the congregation of Meadow Creek. Rooted in Scripture, nurtured by God's Providence, the members of Meadow Creek are related not only by the blood of Christ, but also by the blood of family.

Martin Waddell and Robert Allen fought in the Revolutionary War. Members of the Cochran, Gregg, and Birdwell families also fought in the war. They received payment for their service not with cash, but with land. So this first American generation became the pioneers in the First Frontier. They opened up the wilderness and passed it on to their descendants. Their children and grandchildren were instrumental in the founding of Meadow Creek Presbyterian Church.

It is also important to remember that these veterans also brought their values and beliefs to the wilderness. They wanted new economic opportunities, not a new way of life. From the beginning, there were well-educated leaders who immediately began teaching the next generation.

These stories have been passed down through the generations. The following pages tell those family stories.

From Samuel Cochran to Charles Love: 200 Years of Service and Devotion

Samuel Cochran left quite a legacy. With his first wife, Mary Ann, he built their home near a creek that flowed into the Nolichucky River. Together they worked the land. Together they worshipped at Meadow Creek Academy and Timber Ridge. They had four children, although both Mary Ann and their infant daughter, Caroline died in 1846. Samuel probably buried them near the oak tree that stood on the highest hill overlooking his home. He marked their graves with simple stones. With three children to raise, Samuel married Eliza Jane Hale, a woman twenty years his junior, in 1847. Samuel and Eliza had seven children; however, two of their sons died as infants and were also buried near the oak tree.

Two of his five daughters married sons of the Kiser family, his oldest daughter, Martha married a Russell, Mary Ann married a Taylor, and Margaret married Samuel Love, the great-grandfather of Charles Love. The oldest son of Samuel and Eliza Cochran was James "Alf" Cochran, a beloved elder and Sunday School teacher of Meadow Creek. Samuel Cochran's children, grand-children, and great-grandchildren have always held positions of leadership within the congregation for all of its 200 years. Many of them rest under the oak tree in the churchyard.

Samuel Cochran was the son of a Revolutionary War veteran and it was likely that he attended Meadow Creek Academy, as he was only twelve when it was started. Twenty-five years later, in 1837, Samuel Cochran worked with Marshall Gregg and Michael Woods to organize Meadow Creek Presbyterian Church. Early in the 1840s, Samuel set aside some of his land so that the congregation of Meadow Creek Presbyterian Church could build a meeting house. The small family cemetery he started remains well cared-for today.

Samuel Cochran's legacy was not just the little church he fostered. More importantly, his legacy includes the example that he set and values that he taught his family. He served as an elder for over fifty years. His son Alf served as a deacon for over thirty years. Samuel's grandson-in-law, J.

A. Kiser, served as elder and clerk of the session for many years. Samuel's granddaughters, Jennie and Lucy Russell, led the women's work with the orphans at Grandfather Mountain Home. His great-great grandson, Charles Love spent almost every year of his adult life as either an elder or deacon.

Samuel died in 1887 and in 1894 the congregation published this memorial of him into the Session book:

> *Whereas God in His alwise (sic) providence saw fit on the 7th day of August 1887 to remove from this church our Father, Brother and Friend Samuel Cochran. Therefore be it resolved that the following record of his life and character be spread upon our minutes.*

> *He became a member of this church June 3rd, 1837 his walk in life was that of a true Exemplary Christian character was ever found at his post, ready to perform such Christian duties as laid upon him. He performed faithfully his duties as an Elder of this Church for many years and when called away left that comforting evidence that he had a home not made with hands, eternal in the heavens. He died at his home in the 87th year of his age. His loss was greatly felt but realize that such was his eternal gain.*

Samuel's beloved wife, Eliza, died on December 29, 1910. Her obituary in the Journal and Tribune told her story:

> *Mrs. Eliza Cochrane (sic) died very suddenly yesterday morning at the home of her daughter, Mrs. Kiser, in Greeneville. She was probably the oldest woman in the county, and she and her friends were preparing to celebrate the 91st anniversary of her birth which would have occurred in a few days. She was apparently in perfect health for a woman of her age. After doing some of the house work, she took a seat in her rocking chair taking her Bible in her hand when suddenly and without the least complaint, she leant forward and died in the chair. Her remains were taken to Meadow Creek church on the south side of the river and near where she spent the greater part*

of her life, for burial. She was the widow of Samuel Cochran, who has been dead a number of years.

There are many things that can't be known about Samuel, Mary Ann, and Eliza. Public records document the boundaries of their farm. But there are no documents that tell about their lives. There are no pictures of Samuel and Mary Ann, and the few pictures of Eliza were taken when she was an old woman. Some clues about Samuel and Eliza can be gleaned from the obituary of their daughter, Elizabeth Cochran Kiser: (1939)

> *Her father was one of the charter members of the Meadow Creek Presbyterian Church, and assisted in building of the original church. He raised his family in the very shadow of the church after the strict old blue stocking Presbyterian manner, and his children early identified themselves with the church, so Mrs. Kiser became a devout Presbyterian in early girlhood.*
> (Source: Ancestry.com, Obituaries collected by June Coker McNew, 2010)

Few people in the 21st Century who are not familiar with the basic tenets of 19th Century Presbyterianism would know what "strict old blue stocking Presbyterian" means. However, by knowing what it was that Samuel and Eliza believed—the emphasis they placed on studying the Bible, practicing daily devotions, and doing all for the glory of God—it can be known how Samuel and Eliza Cochran lived their lives. Their faith taught them that God always has a plan, words that comforted them when they faced the sorrow of burying two baby boys. They confronted the turmoil of the Civil War, and the deaths of Samuel's brother, George, and all of George's sons with a clear understanding of the evils of which mankind is capable. Even while the details of their lives are not available, their legacy of faith is observable on the professions of faith carved into their tombstones. The brick and mortar of Meadow Creek and the lives of their many faithful descendants testify to their legacy of faith.

Samuel's memorial speaks of his "exemplary Christian character." That phrase implies that Samuel lived a life of obedience to the commandments.

He also gave generously of his land and his time to the church. Eliza died with a Bible in her hands, because reading God's word regularly and faithfully is very important to a "strict old blue stocking Presbyterian."

Samuel and Eliza followed the advice of Solomon in Proverbs 22:6: "Train up a child in the way he should go, and when he is old, he will not depart from it." They obviously did a much better job of that than Solomon himself. They were Covenanters, and they believed God's blessings and faithfulness would extend to the "third and fourth generations." Their children, Martha Russell, Margaret Love, William Cochran, Alf Cochran, John Cochran, Mary Ann Taylor, Eliza Kiser and Alpha Elizabeth Kiser all became "devout Presbyterians" and stayed close to Meadow Creek. William died in the Civil War at the battle of Vicksburg. Alf became the Sunday School teacher who taught the Catechism to Meadow Creek's many children.

Descendants of Samuel Cochran:

Back: *Jennie Russell, Fannie Burr Kiser, *Lucy Russell, *Alpha Elizabeth Cochran Kiser, Washington A. Cochran, _____.
Seated: _____, *Eliza Hale Cochran, *Alfred "Alf" Cochran, James Kiser.
Infants: Jimmy D. Kiser, Wilma Kiser.
* Buried at Meadow Creek.

Alf Cochran was remembered fondly and there were many anecdotes told about him. He was an elder, therefore Alf Cochran had status within the congregation. He was a respected teacher, and he could maintain order. During Sunday services, Alf would sit behind his students and use his walking stick to pop them on the head if they didn't pay attention to the sermon. Alf tried to speak the truth and expected others to do so also. One time, he asked someone in the community if he would be at a church meeting. The man said, "If I'm alive, I'll be there." But, he didn't come. So the next morning Alf spread the bad news about the poor man's unexpected death until that man heard about it himself. He hadn't spoken truthfully so he was prematurely mourned. (Meadow Creek History, 1987)

Samuel and Eliza's daughter, Margaret, married Samuel Love. They too were members of Meadow Creek. They had a large farm along the river. Their son, William married Ida Bell Huff and they had ten children. One of those children, Lloyd Love, was a member of Meadow Creek all his life and his son, Charles Love is the last one of Samuel Cochran's descendants to attend Meadow Creek.

The Love Family Home on Waddell-Love Circle

William McKinley and Ida Bell Huff Love, 1913.
Children: Back: Fanny, Cleo, Ted, Justicia, McKinley, Viva, Willie Belle.
Front: Syrom, Lloyd, Mary Sue.

Charles and Alice Fannon Love

Charles Love has many, many ancestors buried in the churchyard which motivates him to make sure the church "carries on." But Charles is not worried about the future, because he believes that Meadow Creek is "in God's hands, and He will sustain it as long as He sees fit." Charles was baptized at Meadow Creek and in his eighty plus years he's seen some of the bad times that he believes that "make you stronger." Like his great-great grandfather, Samuel Cochran, Charles Love has given over fifty years of service to Meadow Creek, as a deacon, elder, and Sunday School Superintendent. Like his great-great grandmother, Eliza Cochran, Charles knows his Bible. The verses that have guided his life come from Ephesians 2:8-10:

> For by grace you have been saved through faith; and this is not your own doing, it is the gift of God—not because of works, least any man should boast. For we are his workmanship, created in Christ Jesus for good works, which God prepared beforehand, that we should walk in them.

While serving as Sunday School Superintendent, Charles had the difficult challenge of teaching the Women's Sunday School class which included Rachel Waddell, the woman who had taught him when he was just a child. He was confident that she knew more than he did. As deacon, Charles was always thankful that Meadow Creek never had to take out a mortgage to pay for anything. And having served as both an elder and a deacon, Charles knows that elders and deacons don't always see things the same way.

To make his point, Charles remembers one controversy from his childhood. A big pine tree used to stand in front of church. The elders were always after the deacons to clean the pine straw out of the gutters and off of the roof. The deacons just wanted the tree cut down; the elders did not. One Sunday, when everyone got to church, the pine tree was gone, and the issue was resolved conclusively.

Charles Love married Alice Fannon in November of 1953. They eloped to Greenville, South Carolina, and were only together a short time before Charles was sent to Korea. While in Korea, Charles was particularly touched by the many small children that crowded outside of the fence of the army base. Charles and Alice have always maintained a personal interest in all of the children of Meadow Creek. They take the time to get to know them and applaud their individual accomplishments.

Alice has always appreciated the emphasis on Bible Study that she has experienced at Meadow Creek. Similarly, Meadow Creek has always appreciated the desserts she has supplied to all church functions. Her coconut cake is everyone's favorite.

When Charles and Alice eloped and spoke their wedding vows in South Carolina, they had no idea what was required of each of them when they promised faithfulness "in sickness and in health." Dealing with sickness has consumed a great portion of their retirement years. Each of their elderly parents was housebound, and Charles and Alice brought them meals every day. Each of them has had many serious health problems, but no one at Meadow Creek has heard them complain. They have each faced cancer. They each suffer from chronic illness. When either was hospitalized, the other was always at the bedside. Their selfless devotion to each other is an example to all.

Charles Love is the last of Samuel Cochran's descendants to remain at Meadow Creek. As time passed, they moved away, and many attend churches in other parts of the county, the state and the country.

Just as the red oak tree on Samuel Cochran's hilltop still stands tall and strong, Samuel Cochran's personal example and strong beliefs still influence the church he helped to found. His descendants provided generations of leadership to Meadow Creek, but his legacy to the church was always about much more than his descendants. His belief in strong Biblical preaching and Christian education for the youth remains a major emphasis in the church shaded by that tree.

Note: During the editing process of this book, Charles Love passed away after losing his battle with cancer. Just weeks before his death, the congregation presented him with a plague remembering his "exemplary character," and his long years of service to the congregation.

From the Banks of the Nolichucky River: Crawfords, Allens, and Birdwells

The Nolichucky River runs swiftly through Greene County. It twists and turns and frequently floods, because its waters capture the runoff of the Unaka Mountains. People have lived on the banks of river for thousands of years because the bottom lands are so fertile. In the late 1700s, Davey Crockett's father tried to build a mill along the river, and Davey was born at the site (not on the mountain top as the Disney movie claimed). A flood washed away the mill and drove the family away.

After the Revolutionary War Robert Allen, a veteran, received a land grant of 450 acres along the river. He was a widower and settled into a log home with his five children. He then set about finding a second wife and step-mother for his children. He found Martha Kerr (or Carr) who eventually gave birth to four more children. Robert died before Martha, and he named their oldest son, Daniel Allen, as the executor of his estate. Daniel took care of his mother and through shrewd business dealings expanded the estate from 450 to 1300 acres. It became one of the few plantations in East Tennessee. Daniel Allen was also a personal friend of Andrew Johnson of Greeneville.

Daniel Allen's sister, Margaret, married William Crawford. The Crawfords built a log cabin facing the river. Margaret became a charter member of Meadow Creek. The original Meadow Creek Academy building was within walking distance of the Crawford family as Michael Woods was a neighbor of theirs. However, the Crawford's had many legal problems and lost the property to Margaret's nephew and son of Daniel, James Allen, who purchased it from the court house steps.

Daniel Allen lived from 1791 to 1857. In 1813 he married Polly Baker, and they had twelve children, six sons and six daughters. Of their twelve children, sons James and Samuel, and daughter, Nancy Allen, would join Meadow Creek. Daniel himself would join the church shortly before he died. And when Daniel died in 1857, his son, James Allen took over the plantation.

James Allen was an adventurous young man, and in 1840, he undertook an important service for the Williams family of Greeneville, the most influential family in town. Catherine Williams, a Presbyterian, had become disillusioned with Presbyterianism and she and her husband financed the beginnings of the St. James Episcopal Church in Greeneville. They purchased an organ for that church from an organ manufacturer in Baltimore, Maryland, and they hired young James Allen to bring it to Greeneville from Charleston, South Carolina. James Allen drove an oxcart through the mountains, over the Carolina Piedmont and into Charleston, a journey of about 300 miles. He returned with the organ which was installed in the St. James Church. The hand-pumped organ still plays, and it is the oldest church organ in the state of Tennessee.

James Allen also began an ambitious building project. Over the course of many years, he hired local craftsmen to construct a beautiful white home on the banks of the Nolichucky. He named his place on the river, "Allen's Landing," because it was one of the few places along the river where it could be forded by both horsemen and wagons.

Both the Crawford's and the Allen's were slave owners and they supported the Confederacy during the Civil War. And, because of their location at Allen's Landing, soldiers from both sides frequently passed through this land to cross the river. Because they were harassed by both sides, the Civil War was particularly devastating to them. When the war was over, they did not have enough money to pay their property taxes, so their son, James Allen, Jr., sold off parcels of land to raise enough cash to pay the taxes and liens, thus saving the plantation home.

James Allen married twice. Laura Brown was the mother of his children and Mollie Birdwell, a woman much younger than he, cared for him in his old age. Mollie Birdwell was the daughter of Reuell Birdwell, a Unionist. Mollie's brother, Benjamin lived up the road from the Allen's. Benjamin had purchased the Woods land and all of its buildings including the mill on Meadow Creek. Benjamin Birdwell and his wife, Louise, had ten children.

James Allen, Jr., born in 1855, would grow up and become one of the most important post-war leaders of Meadow Creek Church and East Tennessee. He served as an elder and clerk of the session and chairman of the building committee. While chairman of the building committee, he donated timbers to be milled and used in the construction of the current sanctuary. James Allen, Jr. had a temperament and personality that was the opposite of his father's. He was well-liked and very popular in Greene County. He was elected to serve two terms in the Tennessee Legislature, from 1889-1893 and again from 1923-25. James Allen, Jr. also built the first bridge over the Nolichucky River. It was a wooden covered bridge that lasted until the great flood of 1901. That memorable flood not only took out the bridge, but also flooded the first floor of the great white house to a level of about five feet.

James Allen, Jr. was tall and handsome with a full mustache and the bushy sideburns fashionable at the time. He married Elizabeth "Lizzie" Birdwell, but James and Lizzie had no children. In as much as Lizzie's brother, Benjamin Birdwell had a hard time providing for his ten children, Jimmie and Lizzie took in three them: George, Elizabeth and Louise. They also cared for Leo Campbell, a foster son.

Front: Joe Birdwell, Bud Birdwell, Ben Birdwell, James Allen, Jr., William G. Broyles.
Back: Lillie Birdwell, Lou Birdwell, wife of Bud, Lou Birdwell, wife of Ben, Maggie Birdwell
Johnston, Mollie Birdwell Hurt, Lizzie Birdwell Allen, Mattie Broyles. April, 1917

James and Lizzie Allen often entertained Meadow Creek's preachers at the great white house. While staying at the Allen's, Rev. John Ambrose Wood even fell off the second story porch. James Allen served as the clerk of the Session at Meadow Creek and often represented the church at Presbytery meetings. In spite of his very busy schedule, James Allen made time to attend to church matters.

James Allen, Jr. died in 1934 and his adopted children inherited his land. Over time, George Birdwell bought out his siblings. He acquired the great white house at the auction held by his sister, Louise Harrison, and in 1953, moved into the great white house.

George Birdwell and his wife, Gladys Russell, turned the Allen farm into a very profitable dairy business. They sold their milk to PET milk and George also ran a milk route for the company. In the company news magazine, *PET Dairy Chats*, George is quoted as saying, "Selling milk has meant a better standard of living for our family, better furnishings for our home and more good equipment on the farm." Anyone who has been a dairyman knows it is also a seven-day a week job with no time off for holidays. George's success in the dairy business was partially due to the fact that he had four sons to help with the work. Leo, Johnny, Luke and Jay worked with their father to feed and milk their large herd. Gladys was a leader of the Women's Missionary Aid Society at Meadow Creek and often hosted meetings at her home.

George Birdwell died in 1962 and Gladys lived one day past her ninety-third birthday, dying in September, 1998.

When the Crawford's worked the land, it was a self-sufficient plantation whose cash crops were corn and livestock. When James Allen, Jr., worked the land, burley tobacco provided most of the income. George Birdwell, and his son, Jay, ran a profitable dairy business. Now, in the 21st Century, as Greene County's agricultural economy has changed so has the business of the farm.

Jay Birdwell and his wife, Ann, continued with the dairy business until it became too much work them, especially after Pet Milk closed their processing facility. Their three sons pursued careers other than farming, so they had to find new ways to stay productive. Jay and Ann recognized the growing interest in Agribusiness, so they turned the Allen Plantation—Birdwell Dairy Farm into Still Hollow Farm. They converted corn cribs into a craft shop, built a pavilion, and placed cement tables and benches along Meadow Creek and the Nolichucky River. Still Hollow Farm has been featured on a PBS special about Agribusiness and has become **the** place in Greene County to celebrate weddings, hold family reunions, and other special occasions.

Jay Birdwell served Meadow Creek as a deacon and Ann Birdwell helped to write the last church history published in 1987. As descendants of founding families of Greene County and latest residents of the great white house, they are experts on the history of their side of the river. The land originally owned by the Crawfords, then the Allens and now the Birdwells is a Tennessee Century Farm and is listed on the National Register of Historic Places.

George and Gladys Birdwell also had a daughter, Lois, who married Rev. Powers' son, Johnny. She grew up in the great white house by the river and loved riding her horse along the river and over the hills. When she grew up, Lois followed the example of James Allen and her mother, Gladys. After she became a member of Meadow Creek Church, Lois has always made time to teach Sunday School and Bible School, serve as a officer of the Women's Bible Study, and contributes generously to Meadow Creek's bountiful church suppers.

George and Gladys's son, Johnny Birdwell currently owns the land once owned by Michael Woods. He can see the remains of the chimney of Meadow Creek Academy in his cow pasture.

George Birdwell's youngest brother, Charles was also a member of Meadow Creek. Born in 1924, Charles grew up at the Birdwell Mill, just up the road from his brother George's farm. Charles went off to war with the outbreak of World War II. When he came back, he attended Knoxville Business College and a dental lab school in Cleveland, Ohio, on the GI Bill. Growing up along the river and working the land gave Charles a powerful work ethic. He went to school all day and worked at night. When he graduated, he knew how to make dentures and crowns. He came back to Greene County and worked at the Greeneville Dental Lab until he started his own business, the Dental Service Lab in Johnson City. He was in business for fifty-six years and even worked part-time during his retirement almost up until the day he died.

Charles Birdwell met his wife, Joan, at her sister, Charlsie Hawk's house, across Gregg Mill Road from Meadow Creek Church on Christmas night in 1948. Within a week he was actively courting her and they married in 1951. Joan Ottinger Birdwell was born a Lutheran but married a Presbyterian and feels that Meadow Creek has been a blessing to her all her life. They attended Meadow Creek until they moved to Johnson City, in 1960. They always missed their church family and they came back as members in 1990 as soon as retirement gave them more time to make the thirty-five mile journey every Sunday morning. Their two sons were baptized in the church. Charles served as an elder and Sunday School teacher. Joan "filled space in the choir" and was active in the Women's Bible Study. Charles and Joan particularly liked the church dinners. As newly-weds they literally ate "on the grounds." Charles and Joan especially appreciate the friendship and fellowship found at Meadow Creek. Even though they were separated by many miles, they knew who to call if they needed help. In 1965 they had an automobile accident near to Spruce Pine, North Carolina. After calling for emergency help, they also called Rev. Powers who lived in nearby Micaville. He picked them up at the hospital and took them home to Johnson City. Joan, who has attended many different churches, says that "there's no place I'd rather go than Meadow Creek."

Charles Birdwell died in 2006 and it's very difficult for Joan to make the long drive from Johnson City to Greeneville. But, if her son Charlie knows there is going to be a church dinner, he'll make every effort to get them both back to Meadow Creek.

The Nolichucky River has bordered the home of the Crawfords, Allens, and Birdwells since Tennessee became a state. Crawfords, Allens, and Birdwells have worshipped at Meadow Creek Presbyterian Church since services were first held at the Academy Building on Michael Wood's farm. This family tree has been blessed by good water, productive land, and God's covenant promises. Many of them rest in peace under the oak tree in the churchyard.

Birdwell Descendants at Homecoming, 2011:

Front Row: Joan Birdwell, Mitchell Powers, Rachel Crum, Julia Crum, Monika Birdwell (wife of George) with Kerry Birdwell.
Row 2: Charlie Birdwell, Ann Birdwell (wife of Johnny) with Mia Spradlin, Brye Powers (wife of John Stephan), Heath Crum, Mike Crum, George Birdwell, Jean Birdwell (wife of Leo).
Row 3: Johnny Birdwell, Lois Birdwell Powers, Johnny Powers, Jay Birdwell with Lorelei Birdwell, Leo Birdwell.
Row 4: John Stephan Powers, John Stephan Powers.

The Ruperts "Bring Them In"

The Rupert family came to Philadelphia as German immigrants in the 1730s. One son, Robert Erasmus Rupert, made his way to North Carolina. Four generations later, in 1879, John W. Rupert married Mary Ann Shoemaker, a Cherokee Indian whose family had escaped the infamous "Trail of Tears." In 1890, John and Mary moved into Greene County with six children. They lived and worked on the Allen Farm until they purchased their own land. They eventually had a total of nine children. Mary Shoemaker Rupert was a devout Christian and attended Meadow Creek every chance she could. She was the first of her family to join the church in 1897.

John and Mary Shoemaker Rupert.

It's unknown whether or not Mary could read the Bible to her children, but she surely prayed with them and for them. Then Rev. John Ambrose Wood came to Meadow Creek from Del Rio in 1911. According to his daughter, the author Catherine Marshall, he was a dedicated evangelist who conducted several "tent meetings" during his ministry in Meadow Creek. Because of his preaching and outreach, God answered Mary Rupert's prayers. Her husband and the rest of her family would become professing members of Meadow Creek in 1913. Those nine Rupert children would marry and bring their spouses and children to Meadow Creek. Most of them never left and remain at rest in the churchyard: William and Minnie Campbell Rupert, Robert and Bell Stephens Rupert, Myrtle Rupert and William Lauderdale, Lonnie Lee and Gussie Yearwood Rupert, Hattie Rupert and Claude Ward.

Many of John and Mary's grandchildren would move away from Meadow Creek and attend other churches in other states. Among those that remained, Robert Rupert would serve as an elder from 1926-1960. And, as an elder, Robert pledged $560 towards the new sanctuary, a sum his wife was not sure they could pay. Robert's sons, John and Doak remained members all their lives.

John Rupert remembered that his very first paying job was to help clear the land for the new sanctuary built in 1929. Virgil Hawk asked Robert Rupert if ten year old John would help him for $1.00 a day. John "drove the mules to move the dirt while Mr. Hawk handled the scoop." Doak Rupert's daughter, Caroline, is the last of that line in membership at Meadow Creek. This great-granddaughter of Mary Rupert especially enjoys Wednesday night Fellowship and Women's Bible Study.

Other grandchildren of John and Mary Rupert who remain members are "The Sisters," Bernice Ramsey and Florence Hensley, daughters of Gussie and Lee Yearwood Rupert.

Gussie Rupert married Lee Yearwood in 1905. The Ruperts moved into the area in 1890 and the Yearwoods were here since before the Civil War. Gussie and Lee set up housekeeping in a white frame farmhouse with a magnificent view of the mountains. They farmed many acres of hilly land and had eight children. Children were important to farm families in the 1920s because they provided the labor necessary to get all the chores done. However, Gussie and Lee had seven daughters and only one son, so Omi, Bernice, Margaret, Annie, Sibyl, Easter, and Florence had to learn how to work in the fields just as hard as any boys. By the time Henry was born, his big sisters could do just about everything.

Every Sunday, Lee would get up early to make Sunday dinner and pack a basket full of fried chicken and biscuits. Gussie would pick up baby Florence and put her up on his strong, broad shoulders. Lee and the rest of the children would follow Gussie and Florence as they all walked to Meadow Creek. It was a long walk, so after attending Sunday School and church services, the Rupert family ate their chicken and biscuits under the oak tree before walking back home.

They were all there in April of 1929 when the first services were held in the new brick church. In fact, there were so many people there that the children had to sit on the steps in the front of the sanctuary. Rev. Shortridge was the pastor, and the little girls felt like he was "almost God." They especially liked the way he read I Corinthians 13. His reading made such an impression on their young lives that those verses remained their favorite Scripture passage. Its topic, "Love," provided the theme for their long lives.

Florence and her older sister, Bernice, really liked Sundays. It was a day of few farm chores and a day to play with other children at church. They liked Sunday School, too, but they didn't like memorizing the Catechism. They thought that Rev. Rhea gave them too much studying—"he really piled it on us"—but they did what they needed to do. Bernice recited her catechism to Elder Ivan Ward, Sr., and Florence recited it to Mr. Charlie Waddell, making them full-fledged members of Meadow Creek Presbyterian Church. Of the eight Rupert children, Omi, Bernice and Florence remained members of Meadow Creek all their lives.

Not only did they spend all their lives working very hard in the fields, tending cattle, gathering eggs, canning vegetables, and sewing quilts, these sisters also really knew how to love.

Naomi Dama Rupert Ramsey, 1916-2010

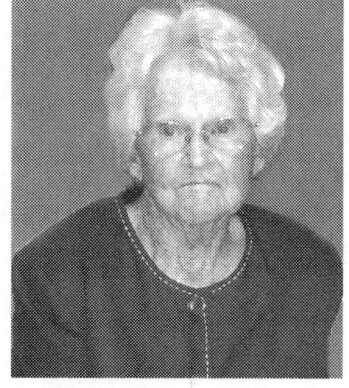

Omi Rupert married Rollin Ramsey and they eventually had five children. They had to bury baby Billy Joe, but Rosetta, Joy, Marty, and Jimmy all grew, married, and made them grandparents. Rollin Ramsey died relatively young so Omi lived many long years as a widow. She showered her love on her children and grandchildren and whatever pastor lived in the manse at Meadow Creek, a home she could see from her front porch.

Omi also loved working the soil and making things grow. She had a magnificent vegetable garden, and her home was surrounded by beautiful daylilies which she frequently divided and shared with other women at Meadow Creek. Her basement was filled with canned tomatoes, beans, corn, and homemade sauces and relishes. Her root cellar was filled with white potatoes, sweet potatoes, onions and carrots. She was only in her fifties when her youngest child left home, but Omi kept working her huge garden. She grew way more food than any one person could possibly eat, so she shared her bounty with the McClellands, Balls, Hartmans, Richters, Longacres, Thorntons, Kennedys and Van Blerks. She gardened until she was almost 90.

By the time the Neikirks moved in to the manse, Omi's family forbid her to work in the garden anymore. Although she was ninety years old, they had to move her into town to keep her hands out of the dirt. To take her place, she asked the new pastor, Jeff Neikirk, to work her land. Jeff and his wife, Carey, understood Omi Ramsey's love of her garden, so in the spring they brought her out to the farm to supervise the planting of the potatoes. They also knew she missed the dirt under her fingernails, so they brought dirt from her fields to town. She carefully planted tomato seeds into that dirt so that the Neikirks could have lots of tomatoes to can.

Omi did not mind the hard work of gardening and canning. She knew she was working along with the Lord in making the earth produce its bounty. But Omi couldn't understand why the Lord took so many of her loved ones and buried them in the churchyard. She and Rollin buried baby Billy Joe; then she buried Rollin; and when her daughter, Joy, died suddenly, Omi's faith was sorely tested. Joy died young, leaving two young sons behind which grieved Omi deeply. She kept asking "why, Lord?" Later, she buried her son, Jimmy, after a long illness. And she lost a young great-grandson because of an automobile accident. By the end of her ninety-three years, Omi was very familiar with death.

Though Omi never stopped grieving for Joy, she eventually understood that sometimes God's ways are above our comprehension. The words of Fanny Crosby's "Blessed Assurance" became Omi's theme song. The congregation of Meadow Creek knew that they would be singing, "Blessed

Assurance, Jesus is mine, Oh, what a foretaste of glory divine . . ." whenever Omi's hand went up during hymn request time. The hymn took on a special meaning for everyone because of what it meant to Omi.

Omi is surrounded by glory divine now. Everyone who knew her will never forget her sparkling blue eyes, perfectly styled hair, and her magnificent garden.

Bernice Rupert Ramsey, 1922-

It is hard to talk about Bernice without also talking about her life-long partner, Ernie. They were inseparable for over sixty years. And it began when her sister, Omi Rupert married Rollin Ramsey.

Rollin's younger brother Ernie became very impressed with Omi's sister Bernice. He thought Bernice was the prettiest of all seven sisters, especially because of her beautiful hair. Ernie spent as much time with Bernice as he could, but in 1942, Ernie Ramsey was drafted into the United States Army. Ernie had never been away from the East Tennessee mountains, and he hated every minute of his basic training in Georgia. When his thirteen weeks of training were over, he told his sergeant, "You can check my bed . . . . I won't be there. But I'll be back."

He made his way back to Tennessee, stayed with Rollin and Omi, and spent time with Bernice. Then, after being AWOL for a week, he reported back to camp and faced the music. His sergeant was angry with him but couldn't punish him, because Ernie had been honest and sincere. He kept his word. Ernie was sent to France and proudly marched down the Champs Elyse after the liberation of Paris. He put in an eighteen month tour of duty, serving as a prison guard for German POWS. He never felt homesick in France, because he knew there was no way he could ever get back to Tennessee from France like he could from Georgia.

Up until the war, Ernie spent most of his life riding farm equipment. To get back and forth from France, the US government transported Ernie Ramsey on both the Queen Mary and Queen Elizabeth. Ernie was discharged in January of 1946 and he got back to Tennessee as fast as he could. He couldn't wait to see Bernice Rupert.

They were married within a year and never separated again. Together they rose at 4:00 am and milked cows. Together they planted their crops, prayed for rain, and preserved their produce. Together they attended Sunday School and worship services at Meadow Creek Presbyterian Church. Together they went to town and every night Bernice prepared cornbread and milk for Ernie's supper.

Ernie and Bernice were married for sixty years. Their love was deep. For over forty-three of those years Ernie never missed a Sunday at Meadow Creek. His perfect attendance set a record that will never be broken. Ernie's faith in God and his commitment to Meadow Creek were very strong. (The photo shows Ernie's perfect attendance pins.)

Ernie and Bernice had a marriage that demonstrated very clearly how two become one. Their teamwork was essential to their success on the farm. And, the love for each other just grew stronger as Ernie's health started to fail, and it became apparent that their time together was growing short.

Mary Hawhee tells of going out to get her mail and seeing Ernie and Bernice slowly walking back towards their home. All of a sudden, Bernice stopped walking, threw her arms around Ernie's neck, and gave him a big hug and kiss. Just a few weeks later, Ernie went to sit out on his front porch while Bernice cleaned up the breakfast dishes. Ernie looked at his farm for the last time, closed his eyes, and left Bernice to go to heaven.

It was almost more than Bernice could bear. But her sisters, Omi and Florence, were still with her. They were all widows now. They all stayed in their own places, but they talked on the phone to each other all the time. Florence drove, so she picked up her sisters every Sunday and they came to church together. They didn't sit together, however. They stayed in the pews that they had shared with their husbands, husbands that now all rested under the tree in the churchyard.

Florence Rupert Hensley, 1924-

Florence was the baby of the Rupert sisters, and as far as Omi and Bernice were concerned, she was spoiled! Florence denied this, of course. In fact, Florence spent a great deal of time proving to her sisters how hard she worked. She competed with Omi in the garden, and she competed with Bernice with her needle and thread. But Florence set the standard in the kitchen. She was sure she was the best cook of the sisters, especially when it came to deserts. Everybody at Meadow Creek wanted her homemade bread, red velvet cake, or apple dumplings.

Actually, all three of the sisters were incredibly accomplished. They could do all the farm chores, because their daddy taught them so well. They were all accomplished quilters and good cooks, because their mother taught them so well. And they were all faithful attendees at Meadow Creek, because Gussie and Lee had insisted on it. When speaking of their parents, they all appreciated that "our mommy and daddy sacrificed to help us get to church." When they each got married, their mother advised them, "Take your Bible and don't lay it down and not read it." So, in each of their homes, their well-worn Bibles were within easy reach.

Florence Rupert married Charlie Hensley in 1946 when he got home from serving in the Navy. Charlie could play the guitar and had a beautiful singing voice, so music was very important in the Hensley home. Florence and Charlie had two sons, Danny and Joe. Danny inherited his dad's love of music and talent for singing. Danny also became a Methodist minister who could preach and sing.

Florence and Charlie were very hospitable and friendly. In fact, Florence's hospitality really impressed David and Ruth Kross when they visited Meadow Creek for the first time in 1999. Florence was at their doorstep after their second visit. She was carrying her special red velvet cake to share with them. She cut the cake into fourths, and gave them one fourth. Omi and Bernice would also get a fourth and she took the rest home to Charlie.

Charlie's kidneys started to fail in 2004. As he grew increasingly weak, Florence cared for him around the clock. She used all her recipes to try to entice him to eat. She tried to keep music a part of his day. As his eyes closed for the last time, Charlie was mouthing the words of his favorite hymn. He sang the chorus in heaven.

Omi, Bernice, and Florence took their membership at Meadow Creek very seriously. The little church has been very important to them for all of their eighty plus years. They kept the catechism books of their childhood and their Bibles were all well read. They raised their children at Meadow Creek and they buried their husbands in the churchyard.

As aged widows, they take care of each other. They share the "Blessed Assurance" of the love of God and the promise of eternal life. Gussie and Lee raised them right.

Florence's Red Velvet Cake:

1 ½ cups sugar	1 ½ oz. red food coloring
1 ½ cups vegetable oil	1 teaspoon vanilla extract
2 large eggs	1 teaspoon cocoa
2 ½ cups self-rising flour	1 cup buttermilk

Dissolve 1 teaspoon baking soda into 1 teaspoon white vinegar

Preheat oven to 350 degrees. Mix oil and sugar, add eggs, beat well. Add food color and vanilla. Sift flour and cocoa together. Add dry mixture to wet mixture slowly and carefully. Add vinegar and baking soda mixture. Mix for three minutes and pour into 3 greased and floured 9-inch cake pans. Bake for 20 minutes or until toothpick comes out clean. Cool completely before frosting.

Frosting:

10 oz. softened cream cheese	1 ½ sticks of softened margarine
1 lb. powdered sugar	1 ½ cups finely chopped pecans (optional)

Cream margarine and cream cheese together. Add powdered sugar and blend well. Add pecans. Spread between layers, on top and sides of cake.
Cake must be refrigerated.

Getting Things Done and Keeping Things Going: The Gammon Clan

Every church needs a family that doesn't wait to be asked to work on a project or complete a task. For Meadow Creek Presbyterian Church, that family is the Gammons. For four generations, members of the Gammon clan have done everything from serving on the Session and Deacon Board to building the Manse, supervising the construction of the Fellowship Hall, to maintaining the cemetery and cleaning the church. They see a job and get it done.

Jack, Boyce, Haynes, Nancy Gammon

Richard and Olivene Gammon came to Greene County from Sullivan County, Tennessee, and settled between the St. James Community and Caney Branch. One of their sons, Landon, married Gaynelle Neas, and they were the parents of Jack, Boyce, Haynes and little Nancy.

Boyce and Leona Gammon

Boyce Gammon married Leona Kiker in 1942. Rev. Wiggins performed the ceremony in the old manse. In 1943, Boyce was sent to the Pacific to serve for over two years in New Guinea and New Britain during World War II. He was a highly decorated soldier when he came home to Leona. They did some farming, but Boyce also spent thirty years working for Kraft Food Company making cheese. He often had to work on the weekends, but he tried to get his work done on Saturday so that he would be free on Sundays to take his family to church. Boyce Gammon served as an elder from 1957-1963 and again from 1969 till his death in 1987. When Rev. Tom McClelland came to Meadow Creek from Ireland, he arrived at the Gammon home with his family and little else. Boyce and

Leona organized the collection of furniture for the manse so the McClellands could move in.

In 1973, Boyce was one of the elders who strongly supported joining the new Presbyterian denomination, the Presbyterian Church in America (PCA), that had been formed. The PCA proclaimed its "loyalty to the Scriptures, faithfulness to the Reformed Faith, and obedience to the Great Commission." For Boyce and Leona, a Bible-believing church was very important. In their opinion, too many churches were moving away from the Word of God.

After joining the new denomination, Meadow Creek needed a new manse to provide for the new pastor, Rev. Larry Ball. Boyce and Haynes Gammon 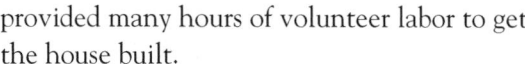 provided many hours of volunteer labor to get the house built.

Leona Gammon played the piano in services for many years. She really disliked playing music with sharps, so she and Virginia Waddell would change hymns with sharps into hymns with flats and nobody noticed the difference. Leona also taught Sunday School and served as Treasurer for the Women's Missionary Aid Society. In 2008, Leona even played the part of the prophetess Anna in the annual Christmas program. Whenever there is a church dinner, Leona can be found working hard in the kitchen.

Boyce and Leona Gammon had one daughter, Sharon. Sharon always enjoyed working with the littlest kids whenever Meadow Creek held a Vacation Bible School. Rev. James Richter married Sharon Gammon to Bill Holt. They were a perfect match as Bill also exemplified the Gammon work ethic. Bill serves on the Deacon Board and Bill and Sharon clean the church every week. Bill and Sharon's daughters, Allison and Kristen, are the fifth generation from the Gammon family who have been born, baptized, and raised in the church.

Glenn and Nancy Gammon Renner

Glenn and Nancy Renner at Meadow Creek 1967

Nancy Gammon came along eleven years after her three big brothers, which meant that on good days, they pampered her, and on bad days, they teased her. Big brothers are like that. In either case, Nancy learned early on how to handle whatever came her way.

Glenn Renner came her way in the 1950s. He was a son of Sibyl Rupert Renner and grandson of Gussie and Lee Rupert. He was raised in the St. James Lutheran Church, but after dating Nancy Gammon, Glenn Renner seriously considered becoming a Presbyterian. They went to Sunday School and Wednesday night fellowships together. The Rev. James Jackson married them. Glenn soon became a deacon and served from 1966-69 and again from 1982-1989.

Glenn and Nancy spent many years maintaining the churchyard. They worked for over five hours a week, using a push mower to cut the grass and hand clippers to trim around the tomb rocks. When the new manse was built, Glenn put up the wallboard and sheet rock. To this day, Glenn and Nancy are the first ones to show up for a work day, and whenever a meal is scheduled for Meadow Creek (which happens a lot), Glenn makes sure there is plenty of ice for drinks.

Nancy has taught Sunday School and served as Treasurer for the Women's Bible Study. Whenever Meadow Creek holds a Vacation Bible School, Nancy provides lots of tasty snacks for the kids.

Nancy also took it upon herself to maintain ties with pastors and their families whenever they left Meadow Creek. She corresponded regularly with the ex-pastors from Rev. McClelland on. When seminarian Joel Kennedy filled the pulpit during the vacancies of 2000-1, and 2007, Glenn and Nancy took a special interest in him and Robin, treating their three children as if they were their own grandchildren.

Glenn and Nancy particularly remember Rev. Jim Richter and his wife, Linda. They became very special to the Renner family and life-long friends. Rev. Richter married their daughters, Louann and Ginger, and helped all the Gammons deal with untimely deaths of Haynes in 1984 and Boyce in 1987. Rev. Richter left Meadow Creek to preach in Biloxi,

Mississippi, but he returned to Johnson City in 2004. So, when Glenn had his heart problems, and was hospitalized in Johnson City, Rev. Richter visited him almost every day.

Like most of the members of Meadow Creek, Glenn and Nancy worked their farm and also took jobs in town. They studied their Bibles regularly and especially liked Psalms 23 and 100. They lived their lives by Romans 8:28: *"We know that in everything God works for good with those who love him, who are called according to his purpose."* Those words took on special meaning in 2004 when Glenn suffered from heart problems and in 2006 when Nancy was diagnosed with cancer. They each endured surgery and long periods of recuperation. Those were very trying times, but they did not give in to despair. They each got better and they were able to celebrate their fiftieth wedding anniversary in the Fellowship Hall of Meadow Creek Presbyterian Church in June, 2009.

Glenn and Nancy's daughter, Ginger, married Mike Ottinger. Mike currently serves as an elder and clerk of the Session for Meadow Creek. All four of Glenn and Nancy's granddaughters were baptized in Meadow Creek. Glenn likes being a Presbyterian so much that he's never missed a service since Jeff Neikirk became pastor. "I get up and want to go."

In honor of their parents, Boyce, Haynes, and Nancy Gammon built the church sign that stands on West Allens Bridge Road. It says simply, "Meadow Creek Presbyterian Church, established 1812. Member of Presbyterian Church in America." It's a testimony to the importance of this little church to the Gammon Family, and for five generations, the Gammons have been important to Meadow Creek.

Descendants of George and Olivene Gammon: Homecoming, 2011

Front: *Patricia Gammon Carter, Nichole Foshie holding baby Natalie, Kari Ball, Alison Holt, Holli Ottinger, Kristen Holt, Sharon Gammon Holt, Leona Gammon, Hope Ottinger, Ginger Renner Ottinger.*
Middle: *Dawn Livingston, Jessica Gammon, Sandy Gammon, Nancy Gammon Renner, Jessica Southerland, Audra Southerland, Bill Holt, Mike Ottinger.*
Back: *Nathan Carter, Scott Foshie, Robert Livingston, Daniel Gammon, Lanny Gammon, Glenn Renner, Louann Southerland, Jeff Southerland.*
Missing: *Megan Haney, Taylor Haney, Jackson Haney*

The Long Line of Long-Lived Waddells

Before Tennessee was a state or Meadow Creek was a church, there were Waddells. Today, there are scores of Waddells in Greene County, and dozens in the church yard. They are the descendants of a young soldier of the Revolutionary War.

In 1763, Scotch-Irish immigrants named Waddell, living in the beautiful Shenandoah Valley of Virginia, had a baby boy they named Martin. Martin grew up fast, and at the age of fifteen, he substituted for Mr. Nicholas Dull as he was drafted to fight at Fort Pitt on the western front of the Revolutionary War. Martin Waddell served for two months at Fort Pitt and then made his way back to Maryland where he was discharged.

Upon discharge, he went back home and kept moving south through the great valley until he ended up near Reedy Creek, North Carolina. In the fall of 1780, at the age of seventeen, he joined the muster of the OverMountain Men at Sycamore Shoals and helped win the great victory at King's Mountain. He was part of the Virginia Militia that left King's Mountain and joined up with General Greene's forces at Guilford Courthouse in North Carolina. Their mission was to capture Tories and return them to General Greene's army. Martin Waddell marched from Hillsborough to Charlotte, crossing the Pee Dee River on Christmas Day, 1780. After returning their prisoners to General Greene, his militia unit was discharged. (Lyndon Eugene Waddell, *Genealogy of Martin Waddell and Descendants*)

Martin Waddell headed west again and became one of the first land-owners in Sullivan County, North Carolina (which would become Tennessee in 1796). Then, in March of 1791, he married Susannah Stokes of Greene County, Tennessee, and settled in the Camp Creek area. Martin and Susannah had one son, Benjamin, and one daughter, Elizabeth. Martin died in 1842, at the age of 79, and Susannah died in 1855 at the age of 87.

Benjamin Waddell married Rachel Bowman and settled in Caney Branch, near Gregg's Mill and the Marshall Gregg family. They had eight children, four sons and four daughters. Benjamin Waddell died in 1878, at the age of 86. The oldest son of Benjamin and Rachel, Washington Martin

Waddell, married Eliza Harrison, fathered seven sons and three daughters, and lived for 84 years. Their youngest son, Jonathan Wiley Waddell, attended Meadow Creek Presbyterian church, raised his children in the church, lived for 95 years, and is buried in the church yard. The four sons of Jonathan Wiley Waddell and his wife, Elvina Bowers Waddell, would provide a lifetime of commitment to Meadow Creek. They also were a very musical group, endowed with a natural talent that they developed without the benefit of formal music lessons.

The Jonathan Wiley Waddell Family at the old homeplace along the Nolichucky River sometime about 1896 or 1897. Dink and Charlie have their fiddles ready for some "Music Makin's." The woman on the porch is unidentified.

Jonathan's oldest son, "Dink," would serve for 37 of his 73 years as an elder and clerk of the Session, and as a trustee. Charlie served 34 of his 83 years as an elder. Robert was a loyal member for 78 years. Decatur became a Presbyterian minister doing home mission work in the Johnson City area and served as a chaplain for the Mountain Home Veterans center. He lived for 85 years.

The James A. "Dink" Waddell Branch

When James A. "Dink" Waddell married Allena Gammon they acquired land within walking distance of Meadow Creek. And Dink spent many hours helping to lead the church in good times and bad. Together they had four children.

James A. "Dink" holding Eloise, Roy, Allena, Chester, and John Martin Waddell.

The oldest son, Roy, eventually moved to Johnson City. John Martin and Chester served as elders and a deacons for many years. Eloise played the piano for Meadow Creek until she and her husband, Fletcher Hagood, left the area in 1945. She lived for 96 years.

John Martin married Rachel Davis who served as an officer of the Meadow Creek Women's Mission and Aid Society. John M. and Rachel had three children: John Martin, Jr., James Edward, and Dorothy.

Dr. Borden and the "boys." In 1896, the "horseback doctor," Dr. Henry Borden, was called out to deliver a baby that would be named John Martin Waddell. It was hard to get to Dink's house because the bridge was out; so Dink met him at the Nolichucky River with a boat and a horse. The doctor made it on time. He often visited with the Waddells in order to play his fiddle with them. They made good music together.

John Martin, Jr., of the seventh generation from Martin Waddell, also served his country. Sadly, he died in an automobile accident as he was coming home for Christmas while on leave from the Navy. The flag pole in the churchyard was erected in his memory. Brother James Edward married Beatrice Swecker. They were members of Meadow Creek and James Edward served as an elder from 1962-65 and as a deacon from 1958-1962. They later transferred to Cumberland Presbyterian Church. Dorothy grew up in the church and often played the piano for Sunday services. When Dorothy married Fred Radar, they remained at Meadow Creek until they moved to town. Fred and Dorothy came back to Meadow Creek in 2010.

John Martin Waddell, Sr., lived for 89 years and his wife Rachel died nine days short of her 100th birthday.

Dorothy Waddell Radar

Dorothy remembers Rev. Rhea walking over to her house many times. He was unmarried at the time and really liked her mother Rachel's cooking. The next pastor, Rev. Wiggins, had lots of children and Dorothy went to school with his daughter, Eleanor. On rainy mornings, the two little girls would wait in the basement of the church for the school bus to come.

Dorothy's Sunday School and Bible School teacher was Nell Hawk, who taught her well.

Dorothy loved her daddy, John Martin, and she still has his fiddle preserved in a special case. All the Waddells played the fiddle even though they didn't read music. Many people from miles around would make their way to the rollicking "Music Makin's" on Saturday nights. Louis Walker would sing, and the Hensleys played guitar. Dorothy still treasures her piano, and she used her musical talents to accompany the singing at church.

She also remembers her granddaddy and daddy reading Scripture and praying in church. Grandpa Dink had physically dismantled the old brick church and led the building committee that oversaw construction of the current sanctuary. Her daddy often represented Meadow Creek at Presbytery meetings.

To this day Dorothy is terrified of fire because her great-grandfather, Jonathan Wiley, fell by the fireplace and died of his burns. Her grandfather, Dink, died in a house fire. But the saddest death of all was when her handsome brother John Martin, Jr., died in the auto accident. Dorothy was the first in her family to learn the news as she took the call from the telephone operator who told her about the tragedy. Dorothy told Fred, who then went for Dr. Cowles to come with them to tell the bad news to her daddy and mother. It was Christmas time, and everyone was anxious to see John Martin again. For Dorothy there has "never been a death as bad to me." Many other members of Meadow Creek still remember that event as one of the saddest times ever at the church, as John Martin was dearly loved.

Dorothy is 83 and bears a striking resemblance to her grandmother, Allena Gammon Waddell.

Tillie Flynn Love Waddell

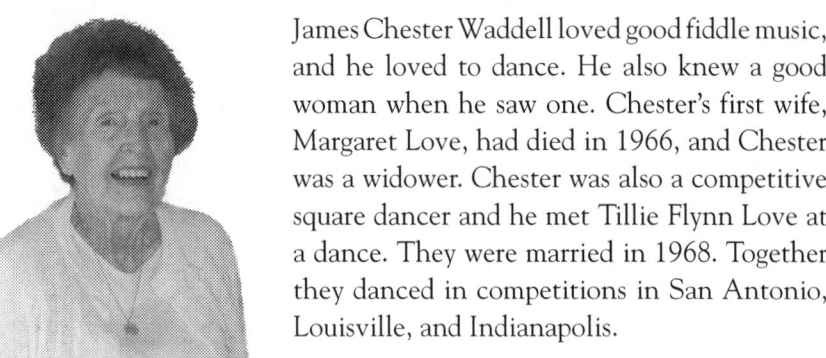

James Chester Waddell loved good fiddle music, and he loved to dance. He also knew a good woman when he saw one. Chester's first wife, Margaret Love, had died in 1966, and Chester was a widower. Chester was also a competitive square dancer and he met Tillie Flynn Love at a dance. They were married in 1968. Together they danced in competitions in San Antonio, Louisville, and Indianapolis.

Chester worked at Pet Milk and was a farmer. Chester always supplied the milk and ice cream for Vacation Bible School. Tillie worked as a nurse at Laughlin Hospital for fifty years. She knew how to do just about everything, from working in surgery with Rosetta Ramsey Wells (daughter of Omi) and Mickey Powers LaRue (daughter of Rev. Powers), to helping deliver lots of babies. She spent most of her career managing central supply. She was so indispensable to the hospital that many times she worked for seven days a week, twelve hours a day. She was paid $50 a month for that service. Tillie was working the morning Dink Waddell was brought to the emergency room, where he died after fire consumed his home and burned him severely. Tillie finally retired in 1991, but only because she wanted to take care of Chester who was suffering from Alzheimer's.

Chester served as an elder at Meadow Creek from 1979-1982 and as deacon from 1971-1977 and 1983-1987. Chester served as a fund raiser for the Fellowship Hall project of 1987. When Johnny Powers worried about having enough money to finish the project, Chester chided him, "Where's your faith?"

Tillie was raised as a Baptist but marrying Chester meant becoming a Presbyterian. Chester and Tillie had a special respect for Rev. Richter, and they often invited him and his family to dinner. However, neither Rev. Richter nor Rev. Neikirk, nor any pastor in between, has been able to answer all of Tillie's questions about matters of doctrine. She loves going to Sunday School, because she learns so much. Chester died on December 5, 2001, his 94th birthday. Tillie celebrated her 93rd birthday in June, 2011.

Great-great-great grandchildren of Martin Waddell, grandchildren of Jonathan Wiley Waddell, and children of James A. "Dink" and Allena Gammon Waddell: James Chester Waddell, Eloise Waddell Haygood, and John Martin Waddell. After serving Meadow Creek for most of the 20th Century, they rest together under the oak tree in the churchyard, a testimony to God's covenant graces. (Photo taken in the 1990s)

Charles Waddell's Branch

Everybody called Charlie Waddell "C. J." Besides being a great fiddler, C. J. could really sing. Throughout most of his years at Meadow Creek, C. J. led the singing in Sunday School, and his strong voice could be heard throughout the sanctuary during services.

C. J. married Bessie Kiser, and they became communicant members on September 15, 1897. In 1926, C. J. and his brother Dink worked with Bob Rupert, Claude and Johnny Ward, and Virgil Hawk to carefully dismantle the old brick sanctuary. It was hard work and many of the building materials were recycled. The wood from the belfry was used to build a shed for Margaret Hawk and many of the bricks were re-used in the new sanctuary that was constructed in 1929. (Meadow Creek History, 1987)In 1926, C.J. was also elected as an elder, a position he held for 34 years.

C. J. and Bessie had nine children that were raised in the church. As they grew up, four of them moved on to other places, but Joe, Ralph, Launa, Ross, and Winnie spent most of their lives at Meadow Creek. Ralph followed his father's example and served as a deacon from 1937-1960 and as an elder from 1965-1968.

C. J. lived for 83 years and Bessie for 80.

Robert Waddell's Branch

William Robert, "Bob" Waddell was the youngest son of Jonathan Wiley Waddell. He and his wife, Hattie Rebecca Rader, were busy farmers along the Nolichucky River. They had one son, William "Delbert," and twin daughters, Betty Jo and Peggy Jane. Betty Jo only lived a few days and Peggy Jane left Meadow Creek when she married. Delbert married Madge Smith and they had two sons, Darwyn and Bobby.

Life along the river was good and working the land was always very important to Bob and his family. Bob died in 1961, the same year as his brother, C. J., at the relatively young age of 78.

Enjoying watermelon along the Nolichucky River with the Waddells: Anna Sue Radar, Darwyn Waddell, William Robert "Bob" Waddell, Bobby Waddell, William Delbert Waddell, and C. J. Waddell. The land that grew these melons is designated by the state of Tennessee as a Century Farm. Jonathan Wiley Waddell originally acquired the land in 1889 and it is now owned by Darwyn Waddell. (Photo taken in the late 1940s)

Darwyn and Virginia Waddell

Young Darwyn was only six years old when the old homeplace burned down and killed his great-grandfather, Jonathan Wiley Waddell. The family saw the smoke in the early morning hours, but it had been burning since about 3:00 am; it was already too late to save either the house or the dear old man. The whole family came together in the churchyard of Meadow Creek to lay him to rest. It was a very sad day.

Darwyn grew up in the church and remembers that Cleo Love Neas was his Sunday School teacher. She taught him Bible stories and talked about the meaning of faith. Darwyn remembers Rev. Beal, not especially for his sermons, but because his son, Howard, became a life-long friend.

One preacher who made a big impact on Darwyn was Billy Graham. Darwyn went to Billy Graham Crusades at Neyland Stadium in Knoxville, and at Madison Square Garden in New York City in 1957, when he was discharged from the Navy. He learned even more about the meaning of faith from Dr. Graham on those occasions. Unlike most of his relatives, Darwyn did not play the fiddle. He only danced a little bit, and did not consider himself a good singer. But in 1960, he married Virginia Self who played the piano and organ and had a singing voice that kept her busy at weddings, funerals, and holidays. Virginia brought all those musical  talents to Meadow Creek. She sang solos, duets with Rev. Powers, and in various choirs. Virginia has been playing and singing at Meadow Creek for fifty-one years.

Like most of his relatives, Darwyn served Meadow Creek as an elder, 1969-1982, and as a deacon, 1964-1968. He was on the Advisory Committee that recommended joining the PCA, and currently serves on the Cemetery Committee. Darwyn believes that Meadow Creek has been a blessing to his family, and his membership is an important part of his life. In his 75th year, Darwyn testifies, "If your Faith is strong, God will carry you through."

Darwyn and Virginia have been guided in their faith by Romans 8 and Psalm 23. Through good times and bad, they can joyfully sing, "Each Step I Take" and "How Great Thou Art."

Shorter Branches

Ebmeyers. Letitia "Cissy" Ebbmeyer and her children joined Meadow Creek in 2010. Cissy is related to the Stewart family and they were instrumental in inviting her and her family to come. Cissy's gift is photography. She has contributed many of the photographs in this book. She and her children especially appreciate the Mission Trips. In the 2010 Christmas program, Eli and Bella had prominent roles.

Front: Haile Stewart, Isabella Ebmeyer, Hannah Stewart, Eli Ebmeyer, Cissy Ebmeyer.
Back: Kaelynn Stewart, Martha Stewart, Brian Stewart, Elaine Stewart.

Mary Hawhee. Mary Hawhee has been a member of Meadow Creek for over thirty years. She and her family moved here from Conshohacken, Pennsylvania. They were friends with James Edward and Bea Waddell who invited them to attend Meadow Creek.

Mary taught Sunday School for many years and has been as affectionate to Meadow Creek's children as to her own two daughters. Mary has also been a member of the Women's Bible Study and took it as her mission to provide flowers to shut-ins and hospitalized members. Mary has an awesome alto voice and provides beautiful harmonies to congregational singing. She always volunteers her talents for special music. Mary has taken care of her disabled sister, Carol Fitzgerald, (a member of Meadow Creek who passed away in December, 2011), and she appreciates the support received from her friends and family at Meadow Creek. Her motto is Philippians 4:13, "*I can do all things through Christ who strengthens me.*"

Hawks. When the Cochrans sold out and moved away, much of their land was purchased by members of the Hawk family. William and Mary Jane Susong Hawk joined Meadow Creek and were the parents of nine children. Their son, Virgil married Stella Bryan and they provided many years of service to Meadow Creek. Virgil was a deacon from 1911-1957, and Stella served as a Sunday School teacher most of her adult life. Their son, Gregg, grew tobacco on the land and married Charlsie  Ottinger in 1935. They raised two daughters in the church, Ginger and Gayle, who moved away when they married.

Of the dozens of Hawks who were members of Meadow Creek, only Charlsie remains, and she is currently the oldest member of the congregation. Housebound at 95, Charlsie credits Meadow Creek with being a real blessing in her life and says wistfully, "I wish I was back at Meadow Creek."

Krosses. David and Ruth Kross joined Meadow Creek in 1999. They are referred to as "Half-backs," a new breed of Tennesseans who were born in the North (Chicago), spent most of their adult lives in Florida, and now have moved half-way back. As city-folks, they had a lot to learn about country living, but the folks at Meadow Creek were patient teachers.

David served as an elder and deacon. He used his skills as a craftsman to renovate the parsonage twice, the downstairs in 2002 and the upstairs in 2007. In 2010-11, he led the renovation process of the church building by re-wiring much of the church, rebuilding walls, and, with help from Pastor Jeff, re-plastering them. Ruth is a teacher and musician and has contributed by teaching Sunday School and playing the piano and organ. A scripture verse that has served as her motto is Psalm 100:1, *"Make a joyful noise unto the Lord . . ."* David and Ruth have always been impressed by Meadow Creek's "dinners on the grounds." Never before, in either Chicago or Florida, have they seen so much good food provided by so few people.

Mohlers. Sandra, Perree, and Gage have always considered Meadow Creek their church home. Contrary to custom, they like to sit in the front of the sanctuary. They enjoy working for Community Day. Five year old Gage tries to make sure he gets either a hug or a handshake from just about everybody each Sunday morning.

Neases. Southern Greene County is full of families named Neas. Descended from German immigrants, they were originally Lutheran and many of them were members of the neighboring St. James Lutheran Church.

In the early 1950s, Rev. Troy Young married Ernestine Neas and Rufus "Rusty" Miller. The Millers joined Meadow Creek Church as it was within

Front: Brent and Kalissa Neas
Back: Todd Neas, Billie Joyce Neas, Jerry Neas, Helen Neas,
Brenda Miller.

walking distance of their home. They buried a baby boy in the churchyard and raised their daughter, Brenda, in the church. Over their lifetimes, Rusty served as a church officer and donated his time and labor to many projects.

Shortly after the Miller's joined, Ernestine's brother, Buford Neas, and his wife, Billie Joyce, joined the church. Buford served as both elder and deacon and Billie Joyce taught Sunday School and sang in the choir for many years. Their two children, Jerry and Sherry, were raised in the church.

Jerry Neas and his wife, Helen, provided leadership to the church throughout the 1980s and 1990s. Jerry was an elder and a deacon and Helen used her musical talents to play the organ and lead the choir for many years. Both of them taught Sunday School and helped to establish Pioneer Groups for the children. Jerry and Helen left Meadow Creek to be church planters in the town of Greeneville for the PCA. They are charter members of Meadow Creek's sister church, Grace Reformed. Their son, Brent, married Kalissa Van Duren in July, 2011, and she is the newest Neas to worship at Meadow Creek. When asked what influence Meadow Creek has had on his young life, Brent said, "Meadow Creek has always been a Covenant family to me. It is clear to see God's grace throughout the generations to this church and families that have been part of it."

Jack and Brenda Neas.

Front: *Pam Bowers, Dustin Neas, Trevor Neas*
Middle: *Lauren Bowers, Brenda Neas, Jack Neas, Sandy Neas, Tim Neas.*
Back: *Ashley Bowers, Brent Bowers*

Jack and Brenda are pretty quiet people. They avoid criticizing and complaining and generally keep their conversations focused on the good things in life. They joined Meadow Creek in 1975 because Gregg Hawk took the time to ask them to come. They raised their children, Tim and Pam in the church.

Now retired, Jack worked at Plus Mark and Brenda worked at Numark. Brenda has a beautiful singing voice and Jack has always helped on work days. Their favorite scripture is Psalm 23.

Thompsons. As a child, Barbara Thompson went to school with Lois Powers. After Barbara married Ken Thompson and they moved to Greeneville, Johnny Powers and Rev. Richter came to invite them to attend Meadow Creek. They joined in 1980.

Since that time, they've always given generously of their time and talents to the church. Ken has served as a deacon from 1985-99 and again from 2002 to the present. He diligently records all the donations to the church and works faithfully with the sound system. Barbara plays the piano for both Sunday School and regular services and only misses her turn when she is sick. They both appreciate the Presbyterian form of church government and the emphasis on Bible study. One verse they especially treasure is Deuteronomy 31:6, *"Be strong and of good courage, do not fear or be in dread of them: for it is the Lord your God who goes with you; he will not fail you or forsake you."*

Other neighbors from South Greene worship at Meadow Creek. The little church under the big tree strives to bring the gospel to its community. Just as it was in 1812, membership is voluntary and welcomed. It truly offers "a historical faith for a new generation," seeking always to glorify God who has provided for this congregation for 200 years.

Roy and Fay Seymour

Sarah and Neysa Mitchum
Patrick Key and Bertrum Seay

Chapter Four

Programs and Plans

For its first hundred years, Meadow Creek served the community primarily as a place of worship. At a time when transportation was so difficult, it also served as a place to socialize. As the second hundred years dawned and people gave up horses for trucks, the church became more focused in its community outreach. Beginning in 1912, a women's group was formed to provide an opportunity for study and service. In 1926, a men's club was formed, although it has ceased to meet. In the 1960s, church members came together to make molasses. Also during the 1960s, the church sponsored a softball team that competed against other churches. The purpose of each of these programs was to bring believers together to work, play, and study together.

Wednesday night Fellowships were begun in the 1970s and have continued since that time. Usually beginning with a potluck dinner, they provided a mid-week opportunity to study the Bible and relevant issues such as "Cults," "Revelations and the End-Times," and other topics of interest. In the 1980s, church members would go on weekend retreats either in Gatlinburg or Ridge Haven, North Carolina.

From the beginning, besides preaching the gospel, Meadow Creek has always had educational opportunities for the children, Sunday School being the most important. In the 1960s, the congregation supported a Boy Scout Troop. In 1985, Pioneer Clubs were provided. Vacation Bible Schools were experienced by three generations of Meadow Creek children. Starting in 2010, mission trips to Jacksonville, Florida, have provided the youth with a week of hard work for those less fortunate, and a time for spiritual growth for themselves. Children's Church occurs when there are toddlers in the sanctuary on Sunday mornings. At various times there have been choirs, vocal ensembles, and instrumentalists. And the Sunday School Christmas Program has always been a big hit.

Beginning in 2008, Meadow Creek has held "Community Day," a time of fun and games to which the whole South Greene community has been invited. Monies raised were donated to the Nolachucky School. The larger community has also attended special services for Veterans Day, Thanksgiving, and Decoration Day. Some churches develop programs that focus on missions, charity, or addiction recovery. Meadow Creek does support missions and frequently contributes to local charities, but its mission is to provide a place for its neighbors in the community to learn more about God through His word and find their special way to glorify Him in their lives.

Current Church Personnel

Teaching Elder ....Rev. Jeffrey Neikirk

Ruling Elders ....Charles Love and Mike Ottinger, Clerk

Deacons......... Bill Holt, Ken Thompson and Stephen Powers, Chairman

Sunday School Superintendent.. Stephen Powers

Teachers ....Carey Neikirk, Elaine Stewart

Children's Church .... Carey Neikirk

Musicians ....Barbara Thompson, Virginia Waddell, Ruth Kross

Cemetery Committee .... Janice Hoyle, Virginia Waddell, Ruth Kross,
Charles Love and Darwyn Waddell

Church Officers, 2010

Front: Mike Ottinger, Bill Holt, Ken Thompson, Stephan Powers
Back: Charles Love, Rev. Jeff Neikirk

Women's Work

"But a woman who fears the Lord is to be praised." (Prov. 31:30)

In 1967, Catherine Marshall's novel, *Christy*, became a best-seller. Catherine Marshall was the wife of Peter Marshall, the chaplain of the United States Senate from 1947-1949. In 1994, the novel was turned into a weekly television series, and all of America became familiar with life in the Tennessee mountains in the early 20th Century. The main character, Christy, was based on Catherine Marshall's mother, Leonora Wittaker. Most of the novel was based on Leonora's actual experiences teaching school in Del Rio, Tennessee and working with the real life preacher, John Ambrose Wood, whose character was named David Grantland in the novel. While the novel ends with Christy marrying the doctor, Neil MacNeil, in real life Leonora Wittaker married the preacher, John Ambrose Wood.

Rev. John Ambrose Wood and his wife, Leonora, left Del Rio and came to Greeneville in 1911. Rev. Wood became the pastor of three Presbyterian churches in South Greene County: Meadow Creek, Cedar Creek, and Mt. Zion Presbyterian churches. Meadow Creek paid half his salary and the other churches each paid a quarter salary. Rev. and Mrs. Wood lived in the Meadow Creek manse, a much more substantial home than their home in Del Rio. In fact, Catherine Wood Marshall was conceived in that manse.

One of the story-lines of *Christy* is the way that Leonora Wood was able to relate to the women of "Cutter Gap." They met regularly and did hand-work while they discussed the Bible, spiritual issues, and children. Leonora Wood repeated that at Meadow Creek and organized the Women's Mission and Aid Society of Meadow Creek Presbyterian Church, founded May 21, 1912:

> *The Ladies of the Meadow Creek congregation met Tuesday, May the twenty-first for the purpose of organizing a Missionary and Aid Society.*

All the ladies feeling the need of such a society in
connection with our church work gave their hearty approval to
the suggestions in favor of organizing. (Minute Book)

Leonora Wood was elected President. A constitution was written which designated the titles and duties of officers, mandated dues of ten cents per month, recommended liberal offerings, and stated their purpose:

The object of this society is to promote the earnest
Christian life and activity of its members, that they may
thereby be witnesses unto Christ in their own neighborhood,
in their own country and "Unto the uttermost parts of the
earth," through such means as the study of the Bible, or
prayer, or religious uses of money, of missions, of personal
religious work, and the consecration of all our strength and
means to our Master's service. (Minute Book)

The members took turns presenting the lesson, devotionals, and readings. On September 10, 1912, they also had the pleasure of "having the mother and sister of our much honored Pastor" visit with them. Usually five or six women met once a month and studied from pamphlets that described the work of Presbyterian missionaries in the Far East, Cuba, and Brazil. They answered the roll call by reciting Bible verses and finished the meeting with sentence prayers. They sent offerings of $6.90 to Japan. In May of 1913, they "prayed earnestly that we may be able to do some definite work for our Master."

Rev. John Ambrose and Leonora Wood left Meadow Creek in 1914. Their daughter, Catherine was born in Johnson City, Tennessee, as they were on their way to a new pastorate in Florida. Without Leonora's leadership, the meetings of the Ladies Aid and Missionary Society tapered off. Although there are three pages cut from the Minute Book, the next mention of the reconstitution of the group doesn't happen until October, 1917, when the new pastor's wife, Mrs. Pearman was elected President.

During the time the women of Meadow Creek were leaderless from 1914-1917, Rev. Edgar Tufts started an orphanage just across the mountains in Banner Elk, North Carolina. The Grandfather Mountain

Home for Children would become the answer to the women's prayer for "definite work," as the orphanage would become their most important and long-lasting charity.

In 1919, Grandfather Mountain Home asked the women of Meadow Creek to take on the support of one child. They pledged to support a young boy named Winston Blair, and thirty dollars were sent over the course of the year. Miss Jennie Russell contributed ten dollars and Mrs. James Allen, Jr., contributed a quilt for his use. On December 30, 1919, the women proposed to ask the deacons to take up a special offering for the Grandfather Home.

That offering was the first of many over the course of decades. They made a faithful commitment of those children. In 1922, they designated their offerings to the "Baby Equipment Fund." In 1923, they held a box supper to raise money for "our orphanage fund." Another young boy named Amos Cole received their support and a quilt in 1925. They raised fifty dollars for him.

For Christmas they worked together with the women of New Ebenezer Church to make up "a nice Christmas Box for the little children at Grandfather's Orphanage."

The Depression of 1929 resulted in few cash offerings. Throughout the 1930s, the women of Meadow Creek gave the gifts of their handiwork: quilts and fruit jars. In 1936, twelve women contributed 150 quart jars of fruits and vegetables. Canned goods and quilts were delivered in the fall, and the empty jars were returned in the spring. The minutes of June 13, 1940, reminded everyone that "fruit jars from the orphanage were on hand and the each one was expected to fill some." By that Thanksgiving, the women contributed five quilts, four spreads, 140 quarts of canned food, two and one-half bushels of wheat, and seven dollars in cash to the Grandfather Home. By 1957, the orphanage was sending a truck to pick up the "fruits, vegetables and canned products" collected and donated to the home. The truck also made stops at Mt. Zion, New Ebenezer, and Cedar Creek Presbyterian churches.

The long-term relationship between the women of Meadow Creek and the Grandfather Mountain Home for Children came to an end in 1973. The orphanage had re-organized but remained with the Holston Presbytery, PCUSA, while Meadow Creek moved to the Westminster Presbytery of the PCA.

With the construction of the new church in 1929, the women added the furnishing of the new church to their fund-raising efforts. On April 16, 1929, the Minute Book proudly notes that the Ladies Auxiliary met in the new church for the first time. They planned a fundraiser to purchase furniture for the church. They made and sold handkerchiefs.

The excellent seamstresses of Meadow Creek spent a lot of time quilting in the 1930s. For a mere $1.73 in materials, they provided the new pastor, Rev. Shortridge, with a beautiful quilt. They enjoyed making that one so much that they immediately set to work on another. In October of 1937, they held a "stork shower" for Mrs. Rhea, the next pastor's wife.

Sometime during the late 1930s, they decided to meet in private homes instead of at church. This decision seemed to cause some controversy, because some members dropped out. It seems that they didn't want to play hostess. There were obviously some hurt feelings. "Those that object to our meeting in their homes are free to tell us they do not want us. Even though we do not meet in your home, don't fail to come to our homes. We will gladly welcome you." Those sentiments did not improve relations as there were no meetings between February, 1938 and June, 1940.

Mrs. Stella Hawk was elected Secretary at that June meeting, and her minutes display her beautiful handwriting. She also wrote joyfully of the fellowship experienced by the women as she ended each entry with the sentence, "A very pleasant social hour followed and tasty refreshments were served."

The reconstituted Ladies Auxiliary was very busy in 1940. They formed a re-decorating committee and proceeded to have fundraisers to re-paint the church interior. There was a potluck supper on the lawn of Mrs. George Birdwell's beautiful home on the river. The most unique fundraiser was the "hen shower." Chicken coops were placed at the church and the Birdwell Mill, and everyone donated hens to be sold to neighbors. They raised $12.15 which was added to the $30 they had already collected so that they could buy "good paint," not "water paint" for the walls.

The meetings of the Ladies Auxiliary opened with devotionals and prayers. Then they took turns offering a topical program. They learned about many foreign countries in which Presbyterian missionaries labored. One presentation was about the Indian Trails of East Tennessee. In July of 1936, Mrs. John M. Waddell discussed marriage, whereupon "a number of the ladies gave their thoughts about married life." They also discussed "Social Obligations," "Stewardship and Christian Giving," and "Prospects and Retrospects."

The women of Meadow Creek raised funds to maintain the sanctuary and the manse, foreign missions, the Grandfather Home, and the Greene County White Cross. They took care of each other with baby showers, birthday parties, and visiting committees. They worked on plays, programs, and church dinners. They had busy hands, curious minds, and generous hearts.

They opened each meeting with prayer and they left each other by reciting the Mizpah Benediction: "*May the Lord watch between me and thee while we're absent one from another.*" (Genesis 31:49) And He did.

During the late 1960s, many of Meadow Creek's women went to work at the many new factories in town; therefore, they had much less time for quilting, canning, and fundraising. The meetings were shorter and focused more on Bible studies and less on missions. Soon they even stopped keeping minute books.

The emphasis now is on caring for the Meadow Creek family. Families dealing with serious illness are supported with home cooked meals. Families that must bury a loved one in the churchyard are provided with refreshments and fellowship after the funeral. And Meadow Creek's church dinners and picnics are famous throughout South Greene County for their quality and quantity. After each occasion, plates of food are provided for shut-ins and widows.

The women of Meadow Creek fear the Lord. They are to be praised by all those whom they love like family.

Keeping the Acorns Close to the Tree

Presbyterians baptize infants as a sign and seal of God's covenant with His people. The baptismal ceremony includes a charge to the congregation to support the whole family with prayer and, for the child, educational opportunities. This responsibility is taken seriously, but how does it work out in practice?

In the 19th century, the emphasis was on Bible Study and making sure the young ones could read the scriptures for themselves. From about 1880-1950, the emphasis was on understanding what Presbyterians believe, so there was weekly instruction in the Westminster Confession, the catechism of Presbyterians. In today's secular world, the emphasis has again shifted to helping young people know how to live as a Christian in a culture that is increasingly hostile to Christianity.

So, even though Sunday School, with its emphasis on Bible knowledge is still very important, there are also opportunities for Youth Meetings at which Covenant youth can talk about problems and brainstorm solutions. Mission trips introduce them to the concept of Christian service.

Finding time for spiritual matters is often difficult for families who participate in organized sports, marching band, while working at a job in town and maintaining farm land. So rather than adding to weekly schedule demands, time is set aside during school vacations for a week of Vacation Bible School, retreats, and service projects.

So, what does this church offer the children? During children's church, the very youngest hear a Bible story and make a craft. During Sunday School, school age children are introduced to concepts such as sin, salvation, providence, and covenant. Vacation Bible School focuses on the complete child and offers music, crafts, activities, and Bible Study. And the mission trip challenges teenagers to use their muscles and sweat for the glory of God.

In 2010, they repaired the home of an elderly woman in Jacksonville, Florida. They worked together as a team to build a wheel-chair ramp for her. In 2011, they built a playground for underprivileged kids.

Carey Neikirk, Pastor Jeff Neikirk, Ginger Ottinger, Aubrey Davis, Elaine Stewart, Hope Ottinger, Stephan Powers, Holli Ottinger, Kaelynn Stewart, Logan Lawson, John Stephan Powers, Hannah Stewart, Jeffrey Neikirk, Mitchell Powers, Haile Stewart.

Meadow Creek's children also contribute to worship services by providing musical selections and special dramatic productions. The annual Christmas program is always a very big event, drawing in relatives and friends from around the county. Every Veteran's Day, the young people place small flags on the graves of the veterans in the churchyard.

But the most important thing the church can do with the children is to love them. So, on any Sunday morning, just before the service starts, the very youngest traipse through the aisles, exchanging greetings and getting hugs and kisses. Everyone's birthday is celebrated, graduates receive gifts and acknowledgement, and teenagers are teased. When they're all grown up and ready to marry, they get a "Pounding," a bridal shower that focuses on supplying the basics such as a pound of sugar, a pound of coffee, and a pound of flour.

When their first child is born, the baby is baptized and it all starts over again. If the goal is to keep the acorns close to the tree, the best way to do it is to:

> *"Train up a child in the way he should go, and when he is old, he will not depart from it." (Proverbs 22:6)*

Haile and Brian Stewart   *Hope and Mike Ottinger*

The Gator Train moves forward . . . .All aboard!
Community Day, 2009,

Afterword

Perhaps the reader thinks that using an oak tree as a metaphor for a church is too simplistic or too obvious. The reason the tree in the churchyard was so compelling to me was because of its size, age, location, and symmetry.

It is a massive tree in a region known for its beautiful tree-covered mountains and tree-lined streets. The original pioneers encountered trees such as this everywhere they went. The whole region was a massive old-growth forest with an incredible variety of hardwoods. As settlers moved in, they used those trees for shelter and fuel and the old trees rapidly disappeared. The red oak in Meadow Creek's churchyard was just a sapling at the time and it survived. A forest service agent confirmed its age, so it is a living link to the pioneer era.

The tree is located between the cemetery and the sanctuary, between those who have died and those who carry on. It is a boundary between the past and present and it shades both. As I learned more about the people of Meadow Creek, I wondered about the multitude of conversations that took place under that tree. I wanted to know as many life stories as I could.

Because the tree so dominates its location and has no competition from other trees, its branches go off in all directions. Its symmetry adds to its beauty, and some of the branches of the tree are so thick and so long that if they were vertical, they would be impressive trees in and of themselves. To me, they represented the families that built and maintained the church. It is rare in America to find Christians so rooted in the land of their forefathers and in the faith of their fathers. These people valued stability rather than mobility. They cherished the eternal truths of the scriptures rather than transient intellectual fads or movements. They wrote freely of their faith and they worked diligently to pass it on from one generation to another. They intuitively understood what each Christian needs to always remember—without Christian education for the young, we are only one generation away from Godlessness.

The two main themes of the book, God's Providence and God's Covenant Promises, are vividly displayed in the churchyard. Man's days are limited, God's promises are not. There are many testimonies of faith inscribed on the tomb rocks, and covenant families are buried together. In America today, death has been removed from the church and entrusted to funeral homes and commercial cemeteries. But churches with adjacent cemeteries are weekly reminders that our lives are in God's hands and under His care. And we can look forward to reunions with those that have died, when the congregation in the churchyard worships with the congregation in the sanctuary before the throne of God.

Finally, since the church is truly the family of God, then publishing the family tree is the most natural thing to do.

Pastors of Meadow Creek Presbyterian Church

Name	Years	Notes
Nathaniel Hood	1837	Appointed by Presbytery
Samuel Gregg	1837-1843	Son of John Gregg
John R. King	1843-47, 1868, 1884	
Francis Allison McCorke, MD	1844, 1847-48	
Jacob Hood	1850	
Ira H. Morey	1853-56	
Alexander Adams Blair	1859	
J.M. Huffmeister	1860	
John Nelson Blackburn	1862, 1865	Driven out by Unionists
David F. Palmer	1867-68	Died unexpectedly
George Aiken Calwell	1869, 1876	
James Polk Doggett	1900-1907	
James Alexander Thompson	1909-1911	
John Ambrose Wood	1911-1914	Father of Catherine Marshall
Bruce Bridwell Shankel	1915	
Henry Harrison Cassady	1916	
William Thomas Pearman	1917-1920, 1925-1927	
John Martin	1920-1922	
Douglas Clark Amick	1928	
Roy Lee Shortridge	1929-1936	
John Irvin Rhea	1936-1939	
Cecil Matthews Brown	1940-1942	
Birl Herman Wiggens	1942-1945	
Edward Leyburn Beall	1945-1947	
Jack Fleck	1951-1952	
Troy Lyda Young	1953-1955	
James Everett Jackson, Jr.	1956-1958	
John S. Powers	1960-1964	
Richard LeVern White	1967-1969	
Thomas McClelland	1969-1973	

Larry Ball	1973-1977
Richard Rosser	1978
Lauren Stanley Hartman	1978-1981
James E. Richter	1982-1989
David Longacre	1990-1992
James Thornton	1993-2000
Joel Kennedy	2000-01, 2007-8
Jan Theoron Van Blerk	2002-2007
Jeffrey Neikirk	2008-Present

Elders

The elders are elected by the congregation. They serve as a Session and conduct the business of the church, in matters of preaching, teaching and finance. Elders generally serve from the time of ordination until their death. In the 1960s a three-year rotation system was developed which was changed again in the 1990s. The first date is the date given for installation or ordination. If there is no ending date, he served until his death.

Dates	Names
1837	John Gregg
	John Dunlap Jacob Kelly
	Samuel Cochran
1841-49	William Grace
1844	Marshall Gregg
	Samuel D. Nelson
	Samuel Henry
1878	David Leonidas Woods
1892	James A. Kiser
1892-97	Thomas S. Snapp
1894	John Bowers
1897-98	James Allen, Jr.
1897	James Alexander
1902	Nathaniel Chambers
1911	James A. Waddell
	James Allen, Jr.
1918	Horace N. Bower
	C. J. Waddell
	Grady Kiser
1926-60	Robert Rupert
1926-35	Fred Gray
1926-40	Ivan Ward, Sr.
1937	Clay Neas
1947-54	Ottis Harrison
1947	Tom Tweed
1947-60, 62-65, 67-71	John M. Waddell

1957-63, 69-87	Boyce Gammon
1957-60	Ralph Lewis Waddell
1960-63	Charles Birdwell
	Gregg Hawk
1960-63, 65-68, 70-79	Ralph Waddell
1962-65	W. Buford Neas
1962-65, 71	Gray Nease
1964-67, 71-75	Paul Hensley
1964-73, 79-89, 91-2000, 2002-Present	Charles Love
1965-69, 73-82, 95-2001	Ivan Ward, Jr.
1966-69, 73-83	Haynes Gammon
1967-71	Lloyd Love
1969-82	Darwyn Waddell
1977-81	Richard Nesbitt
1979-82	Chester Waddell
1981-84	Henry Terrell
1983-89, 91-99	Jerry Neas
1987-99	Jim McGowan
1990-93	Lanny Gammon
1999-2000	Louis Calabrisi
2002-05	David Kross
2002-05	John Powers
2002-Present	Mike Ottinger

Deacons

Deacons are elected by the congregation to tend to the needs of the congregation and manage the sanctuary and grounds. Their terms varied over the years and the records are not always clear. New elections are recorded, but retirements are not. And, they didn't record members of the office for the first twenty-five years. This list therefore is not completely accurate.

Dates	Names
1862	Daniel Cooper
Joel	Bowers
1892	James Alfred Cochran
	Joel Bowers
1892-97, 98-1911	James Allen, Jr.
1902-48	W. K. Mitchell
1911-14	W. A. Houston
1911-1957	Virgil Hawk
1916-26	Robert Rupert
1926-47	Ottis Harrison
	John M. Waddell
1926-35	Hubert Renner
	John Russell
1937-57, 63-66, 1969-1974	Gregg Hawk 1937-60 Ralph Waddell
1940-61	Lloyd Love
1949-58	Gray Nease
1949-58	Hugh Foreman
1949-62, 69-79	Clarence Hawk
1958-62, 66-69	W. Buford Neas
1958-62, 60-64	James Edward Waddell
1960-64, 73-79	Charles Love
1960-63	Rufus Miller
1961-64	Johnny Rupert
1961-64, 70-73	Ivan Ward, Jr.
1962-65, 67-71	Harold Love
1962-67	Billy Gray Neas

1963-65	Leo Birdwell
1964-68	Darwyn Waddell
1964-67	Boyce Gammon
1965-68	Doak Rupert
1965-68, 70-73	Douglas Malone
1966-69, 82-87, 89-95	Glenn Renner
1967-71	Paul Hensley
1971-86, 92-94	Jay Birdwell
1971-77, 83-88	Chester Waddell
1973	Daniel Hensley
1975-82	Jerry Neas
1977-81	Charles Hensley
1979-88, 91-99	John Powers
1985-99, 2002-Present	Ken Thompson
1986-89	Lanny Gammon
1989-95	Don Wilhoit
1996-99	Mike Johnson
2000-02	David Kross
2002-Present	Bill Holt
	Stephen Powers
2004-06	Brian Neas

Bibliography

Bible, Mitzi V. *Community in Transitions: Greene County Tennessee, 1865-1900*. Knoxville, TN. East Tennessee Historical Society's Community History Program. 1986.

Burgner, Goldene Fillers. *The Southside*. Self-Published, 1977.

Corlew, Robert E. *Tennessee: A Short History*, 2nd edition. Knoxville: The University of Tennessee Press, 1999.

Crawford, Earle W. *Samuel Doak: Pioneer Missionary in East Tennessee*. Johnson City: The Overmountain Press, 1999.

Doughty, Richard. *Greeneville: One Hundred Year Portrait, 1775-1875* Self-Published.

Dykeman, Wilma. *Tennessee: A History*. Newport TN: Wakeston Books, 1984.

Greene County History Book Committee. *Historic Greene County, Tennessee, and It's People, 1783-1992*. Waynesville, NC: Walsworth Publishing, Don Mills, Inc., 1992.

Kennedy, Billy. *The Scots-Irish in the Hills of Tennnessee*. Londonderry and Belfast: Causeway Press, 1995.

Members of Timber Ridge Church. *Timber Ridge Church: A 200 Year Heritage of Presbyterian Faith, 1786-1986*. Rogersville, TN: East Tennessee Printing Co., Inc., 1986.

Members of Meadow Creek. *Meadow Creek Presbyterian Church*. Greeneville, TN., Self-Published. (Printed in 1987)

Roberts, Harry B. *Olden Times in Greene County, Vol. 1*. Self-published, 1983.

Sandburg, Carl. *Abraham Lincoln, the War*, Vol. 1. New York: Harcourt Brace and Co. 1939.

Unpublished Sources:

Bridgeforth, William. *The Genealogy of the Cochran Family*

Court records: State of Tennessee vs. Rankin Houston, W. A. Houston, March 23, 1915.

Harmon, Katherine Susong. *Robert Cochran Family: Civil War Letters, Cochran Bible Records, Settlement of Estate.*

———— *Research on the East Tennessee Nolichuckey River: Thomas Love, Esq. Families.*

———— *Jonathan & Hannah Cravens Evans of Nolichuckey River Area*

Waddell, Lyndon. *Descendants of Martin Waddell.*

Land Records and Title deeds: Greene County Tax Assessors Office.

Author's Note: The history of the Civil War in the mountain South is not as widely known as the great battles that took place, but it was truly a horrible time. If the reader is interested in learning more about it, there are some excellent accounts available:

Philip Shaw Paludan's *Victims: A True Story of the Civil War*, (Knoxville: The University of Tennessee Press, 1997) and William R. Trotter's *Bushwackers: The Civil War in North Carolina, The Mountains*, (Winston-Salem: John F. Blair Pulisher, 1988) are the most compelling accounts. Trotter's book includes a chapter on the Shelton Laurel Massacre an event that took place not far from Greeneville, TN.